HEALTH CARE ISSUES, COSTS AND ACCESS

HIGH RISK HEALTH INSURANCE POOLS

HEALTH CARE ISSUES, COSTS AND ACCESS

Additional books in this series can be found on Nova's website under the Series tab.

Additional e-books in this series can be found on Nova's website under the e-book tab.

HEALTH CARE ISSUES, COSTS AND ACCESS

HIGH RISK HEALTH INSURANCE POOLS

JENNY ALVAREZ
EDITOR

New York

For permission to use material from this book please contact us:
Telephone 631-231-7269; Fax 631-231-8175
Web Site: http://www.novapublishers.com

Library of Congress Cataloging-in-Publication Data

ISBN: 978-1-62417-421-6

Published by Nova Science Publishers, Inc. † New York

CONTENTS

PREFACE

Since 1975, a growing number of states have implemented high risk pools (HRPs), which offer nonprofit health insurance to individuals who are unable to purchase affordable coverage in the private market because of preexisting conditions. State HRPs often contract with a private health insurance carrier to administer the pool, and plan options can vary significantly both within pools and from state to state. This book examines the temporary federal high risk pool (HRP) program, also known as the Pre-Existing Condition Insurance Plan (PCIP); with a focus on enrollment, benefits and funding.

Chapter 1 – This chapter briefly describes the temporary federal high risk pool (HRP) program, more commonly known as the Pre-Existing Condition Insurance Plan (PCIP) program. The PCIP program was established by the Patient Protection and Affordable Care Act (PPACA, P.L. 111-148, as amended). Under PPACA, the PCIP program is intended to help individuals with preexisting conditions who have been uninsured for six or more months to obtain health insurance coverage before 2014. In 2014, coverage will be available on a guaranteed issue basis and preexisting condition exclusions will be prohibited.

To be a qualified PCIP, the insurance coverage must have an actuarial value (the average percentage of expenses that the plan covers) at least equal to 65% of total allowed costs, and out-of-pocket costs cannot exceed $5,950 for an individual in 2011. The premiums must be established at a standard rate for a standard population, and age rating cannot exceed a factor of 4 to 1. Claims and administrative costs will be subsidized by the federal government.

Chapter 2 – This is Statement of Steven B. Larsen.

Chapter 3 – In an effort to expand the options for health coverage, 35 states have established high risk health insurance pools. These programs target individuals who cannot obtain or afford health insurance in the private market, primarily because of preexisting health conditions. Also, many states use their high risk pools to comply with the portability and guaranteed availability provisions of the Health Insurance Portability and Accountability Act of 1996 (P.L. 104-191).

In general, state high risk pools tend to enroll a small percentage of the uninsured. In December 2009, approximately 208,000 individuals were enrolled in high risk pools. State-established nonprofit organizations typically run these pools, with private insurance companies handling day-to-day operations, along with plan administrative staff. Although benefit packages vary across states and plans, they generally reflect health benefits that are available in the private insurance market. The majority of high risk pools cap premiums between 150% to 200% of market rates, and pools are subsidized through insurer assessments and other funding mechanisms.

Chapter 4 – A growing number of states—35 as of June 2009—have created high-risk health insurance pools (HRPs) primarily to provide coverage to individuals whose health status limits their access to coverage in the private individual health insurance market. HRPs—typically state-run nonprofit associations—often contract with a private health insurance carrier to administer the pool and offer a range of health plan options to such individuals, who are commonly referred to as medically uninsurable. Plan options vary within pools and from state to state, and like the private individual market, HRPs typically impose waiting periods for coverage of preexisting conditions to discourage medically uninsurable individuals from foregoing health insurance until they require care.

In: High Risk Health Insurance Pools
Editor: Jenny Alvarez
ISBN: 978-1-62417-421-6

Chapter 1

TEMPORARY FEDERAL HIGH RISK HEALTH INSURANCE POOL PROGRAM*

Mark Newsom

SUMMARY

This chapter briefly describes the temporary federal high risk pool (HRP) program, more commonly known as the Pre-Existing Condition Insurance Plan (PCIP) program. The PCIP program was established by the Patient Protection and Affordable Care Act (PPACA, P.L. 111-148, as amended). Under PPACA, the PCIP program is intended to help individuals with preexisting conditions who have been uninsured for six or more months to obtain health insurance coverage before 2014. In 2014, coverage will be available on a guaranteed issue basis and preexisting condition exclusions will be prohibited.

To be a qualified PCIP, the insurance coverage must have an actuarial value (the average percentage of expenses that the plan covers) at least equal to 65% of total allowed costs, and out-of-pocket costs cannot exceed $5,950 for an individual in 2011. The premiums must be established at a standard rate for a standard population, and age rating cannot exceed a factor of 4 to 1. Claims and administrative costs will be subsidized by the federal government.

States can run the program or elect to have the Department of Health and Human Services (HHS) operate the program in their states. Slightly more than

* This is an edited, reformatted and augmented version of the Congressional Research Service Publication, CRS Report for Congress R41235, dated June 13, 2011.

half of states (27 states) contracted to operate their own PCIPs. HHS administers the PCIPs in 23 states and the District of Columbia. PPACA appropriates $5 billion of federal funds to support the program, available from July 1, 2010, until the program ends on January 1, 2014. Originally projected to have 200,000 or more enrollees, the PCIPs had 21,454 enrollees as of April 30, 2011. This is a 168.65% increase from the first enrollment statistics released on November 1, 2010.

INTRODUCTION

Since 1975, a growing number of states (35 currently) have implemented high risk pools (HRPs), which offer nonprofit health insurance to individuals who are unable to purchase affordable coverage in the private market because of preexisting conditions.[1] State HRPs often contract with a private health insurance carrier to administer the pool, and plan options can vary significantly both within pools and from state to state.[2] The Government Accountability Office (GAO) estimates that nearly 4 million individuals were eligible in states with HRPs between 2005 and 2007.[3] However, in 2008, only a total of 199,020 individuals (ranging from 300 in Florida to 27,386 in Minnesota) were enrolled in the 34 HRPs in operation during that time.[4] The National Association of State Comprehensive Health Insurance Plans (NASCHIP) believes that the limited funding to subsidize the relatively high premiums charged for HRPs has restrained enrollment in the plans.[5]

The Patient Protection and Affordable Care Act (PPACA, P.L. 111-148, as amended) requires the Secretary of Health and Human Services (hereafter the Secretary) to establish a temporary federal HRP program to provide access to uninsured individual with preexisting conditions. Under PPACA, the federally financed HRP program is intended to help certain individuals with preexisting conditions obtain coverage for the period between June 23, 2010 (functionally the July coverage month) and January 1, 2014.[6]

TEMPORARY FEDERAL HIGH RISK POOL PROGRAM

The temporary HRP program, or the Pre-Existing Condition Insurance Plan (PCIP) as it is commonly referred to, is intended to provide transitional coverage for uninsured individuals with preexisting conditions until January 1,

2014, when group health plans and health insurance issuers of group or individual health insurance coverage will be prohibited from having preexisting condition exclusions.[7] Also effective for 2014 is the "guaranteed issue" provision requiring health insurance issuers in the individual or group market to be available to every employer and individual in the state that applies for coverage.[8] Thus, individuals with preexisting conditions should not require a PCIP on or after January 1, 2014, because they will have access to health insurance coverage in the reformed insurance marketplace.

A PCIP can be administered either by a state or by the U.S. Department of Health and Human Services (HHS). The HHS-administered PCIPs are operated by the Government Employees Health Association, Inc. (GEHA), a non-profit insurance carrier.[9] States that administer their own PCIP may use a different name and insurance carrier. For example, North Carolina named their PCIP "Inclusive Health: Federal Option," and the pool is operated by the North Carolina Health Insurance Risk Pool, Inc., a state sponsored non-profit organization.[10] As illustrated in **Figure 1**, slightly more than half of the states (27) have accepted responsibility for administering their own PCIP plan, while 23 states and the District of Columbia (DC) requested that HHS run the program on their behalf. A list of PCIP websites is available in **Table A-1**.

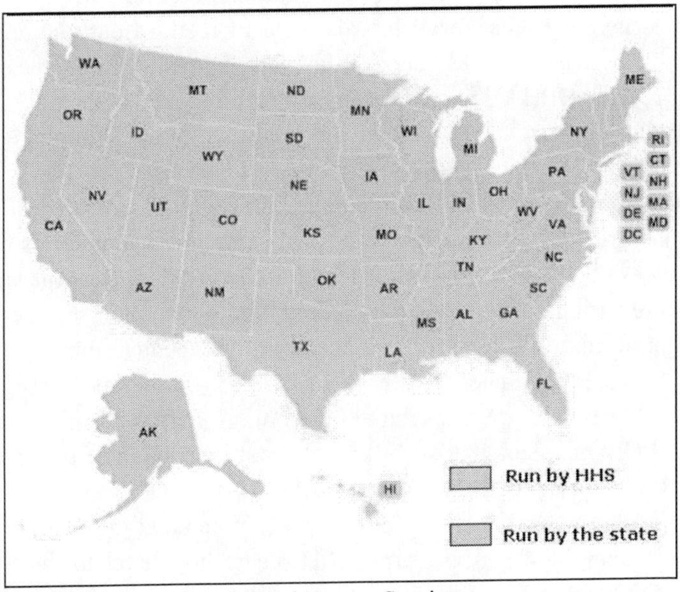

Source: U.S. Department of Health and Human Services.

Figure 1. Map of PCIPs Administered by the States or HHS.

Program Administration

PPACA provides that the Secretary may carry out the federal HRP program directly or through contracts to eligible entities.[11] In order to carry out the program, and other PPACA private health insurance provisions, the Secretary created a new Office of Consumer Information and Insurance Oversight (OCIIO) within the Office of the Secretary (OS).[12] Within OCIIO, the Office of Insurance Programs (OIP) was established to be responsible for administering the temporary high risk pool program and associated funding to states. Richard Popper, who previously directed the state of Maryland's high risk pool, was appointed the director of the OIP.[13] On January 26, 2011, OCIIO was reorganized as the Center for Consumer Information and Insurance Oversight (CCIIO), a component in the Centers for Medicare and Medicaid Services (CMS).[14] Steve Larsen currently serves as the Deputy Administrator and Director of CCIIO, and the OIP is now the Insurance Programs Group, still under the direction of Richard Popper.[15]

Funding for Eligible Entities

To be eligible to contract with the Secretary for the PCIP, an entity must either be a state or nonprofit private organization.[16] For the other 23 states and DC, HHS issued a request for proposals for a PCIP third party administrator on May 25, 2010.[17] HHS chose the Government Employees Health Association, Inc. (GEHA), from the 14 non-profit organizations that expressed interest in the program.[18] GEHA is also currently a Federal Employee Health Benefits Program (FEHBP) carrier.[19]

PPACA appropriated $5 billion to pay claims and the administrative costs of the temporary HRP that are in excess of the amount of premiums collected from enrollees beginning on July 1 2010, until the program ends on January 1, 2014.[20] There has been some concern that the funding amount is inadequate for the program. Richard Foster, the chief actuary of the Centers for Medicare and Medicaid Services, estimates that by 2011 or 2012 the initial funding will be exhausted, "resulting in substantial premium increases to sustain the program."[21] CBO concurs that $5 billion will not be enough to cover the costs of all applicants through 2013.[22]

Many of the states that elected not to participate cited the funding as their reason. For example, Texas Governor Rick Perry in a letter to the Secretary stated that the funding is insufficient and that "state officials could be forced to reduce health coverage, raise premiums or ask state taxpayers to pay" for the

HRP.[23] Similarly, Wyoming Governor Dave Freudenthal wrote the Secretary expressing the concern "that the allotted money may prove to be insufficient to fully operate this program until 2014."[24] If HHS estimates that there will be a funding shortage, then the Secretary has the authority to make any program adjustments necessary to eliminate the deficit.[25]

The Secretary has proposed allocating funds for the program by using a formula similar to what was used for the State Children's Health Insurance Program (CHIP), whereby funds would be allotted to states using a combination of factors, including nonelderly population, nonelderly uninsured, and geographic cost, as a guide.[26] The Secretary intends to reallocate the unspent state allotments after a period of not more than two years, based on an assessment of enrollment and expenditure experiences of each state. A breakdown of the proposed funding by state is provided in **Table A-2**.

Eligibility Criteria

The PCIP program is intended to supplement existing state HRPs. Indeed, existing state HRP enrollees are ineligible for the federal program because federal enrollees must be without credible coverage for a six-month period prior to the date on which the individual is applying for coverage through the federal PCIP program.[27] Credible coverage is defined by §2701(c) of the Public Health Service Act (PHSA) as a group health plan, health insurance coverage, Medicare Part A or Part B, Medicaid, coverage from the Department of Defense, a medical care program of the Indian Health Service (IHS), a state health benefits risk pool, the Federal Employee Health Benefits Program (FEHBP), a public health plan (as defined in regulations), or a health benefit plan under the Peace Corps Act.[28] The criteria is based on enrollment in credible coverage, not on access to it. In other words, PCIPs are permitted to deny eligibility based on an applicant's enrollment in creditable coverage during the six-month period prior to applying for PCIP, but they may not deny coverage to an otherwise eligible individual merely because the individual has access to credible coverage.[29]

Eligible individuals must also have a preexisting condition, as determined by the Secretary.[30] In the interim final rule published on July 30, 2010, the Secretary established the following criteria for determining if an individual has a preexisting condition for the purposes of PCIP eligibility: (1) the individual provides documented evidence that an insurer has refused, or has provided clear indication that it would refuse, to issue individual coverage on grounds related to the individual's health; (2) the individual provides documented evidence that he or she has been offered individual coverage but only with a rider that excludes coverage of benefits associated with a preexisting condition; (3) the individual provides documented evidence that he or she has a medical or health condition specified by the state and approved by the Secretary for inclusion in PCIP; or (4) other criteria as defined by the PCIP and approved by the Secretary.[31]

Finally, eligible individuals must be a citizen or national of the United States or be lawfully present in the United States.[32] To assist in determining citizenship or nationality, HHS is creating a new computer matching program with the U.S. Office of Personnel Management (OPM), the Social Security Administration (SSA), and the Department of Agriculture's National Finance Center (NFC).[33] This program will allow for the matching between agency systems of the following data fields: name, address, date of birth, Social Security Number (SSN), and Tax Identification Number (TIN).

Application Procedures and Enrollment

To apply for the PCIP administered by HHS, eligible individuals must submit an application and supporting materials indicating their eligibility. The PCIP has both paper and online application options available.[34] Prospective applicants can also call to request a mailed copy of the application at 1-866-717-5826 (TTY 1-866-561-1604). The application requires basic personal information, indication of citizenship or immigration status, information about the applicant's medical condition or diagnosis that makes the individual eligible, and information about previous health insurance coverage.[35] PCIP applicants must also supply a copy of a letter dated within six months of the application from an insurance company or health plan showing that they had been completely denied individual coverage because of a preexisting condition, or were offered coverage but were denied certain benefits because of a preexisting condition. Federal HRPs administered by the states may develop their own application procedures, and thus some variation has been observed.[36] Specific state contacts for applications are available at the Pre-Existing Condition Insurance Plan website.[37]

The Congressional Budget Office (CBO) estimated around 200,000 individuals would be enrolled on average over the 2011-2013 period, based on the assumption that HHS will only spend the $5 billion appropriated in

PPACA.[38] However, CBO expects that if the program spending were not capped and 65% of medical costs were covered, then federal spending through 2013 would be between $10 billion and $15 billion and enrollment would be expected to grow from approximately 400,000 in 2011 to as high as 700,000 in 2013.[39] As of the enrollment figures released on February 1, 2011, 12,437 individuals have enrolled in PCIPs (see **Table 1** for PCIP enrollment by state).

The reasons for the lower than expected enrollment have not been independently researched yet. Nevertheless, CCIIO explained in the CMS FY2012 budget justification submission that in the initial months of the program, efforts were focused on establishing the program within the 90-day time period required by PPACA and this compressed implementation schedule necessitated focus on operational matters (e.g., developing claims adjudication, enrollment, and premium collection systems) rather than devoting substantive effort on an education campaign.[40] CCIIO is now working on public education efforts. In testimony before the House Committee on Energy and Commerce, Subcommittee on Oversight and Investigations, CCIIO Director Steven Larsen stated that:

> CCIIO has an aggressive strategy to encourage enrollment of eligible individuals, meeting with local doctors, hospitals, consumer groups and chapters of advocacy groups like the American Cancer Society and American Diabetes Association. For example, we are working to reach local stakeholders and providers who come into contact with people with chronic care needs in need of insurance to spread awareness about the PCIP program. We have actively reached out to provider groups through webinars, arranged meetings with potential partners in at least six States, and will continue this outreach in the coming months. CMS is also working with agencies that have a history serving individuals with disabilities, such as the Social Security Administration. Since February 15, 2011, all applicants for Social Security disability benefits have been informed about the PCIP program through application receipts. These collaborations leverage existing communication channels with individuals who have a pre-existing condition and may therefore be eligible for the PCIP program.[41]

On May 31, 2011, HHS announced that the eligibility standards will be eased to facilitate enrollment in the states where the PCIPC are federally administered.[42] Starting July 1, 2011, applicants may merely provide a letter from a doctor, physician assistant, or nurse practitioner dated within the past 12 months stating that they have or, at any time in the past, had a medical condition, disability, or illness. Applicants will no longer have to wait on an insurance company to send them a denial letter.[43]

Table 1. PCIP Enrollment by State November 1, 2010 through April 30, 2011

State	Date Coverage Began (in 2010)	11/1/2010 Enrollment	2/1/2011 Enrollment	3/31/2011 Enrollment	4/30/2011 Enrollment
Alabama	August 1	33	61	77	91
Alaska	September 1	12	20	32	34
Arizona	August 1	112	270	374	457
Arkansas	September 1	127	147	198	226
California	October 25	513	706	1,543	1,858
Colorado	September 1	368	434	617	699
Connecticut	September 1	12	22	34	42
Delaware	August 1	13	34	41	54
DC	October 1	0	10	15	21
Florida	August 1	293	613	770	925
Georgia	August 1	161	399	515	608
Hawaii	August 1	11	23	24	27
Idaho	August 1	19	42	43	47
Illinois	September 1	664	943	1,150	1,261
Indiana	August 1	63	131	177	201
Iowa	September 1	56	80	129	143
Kansas	August 1	81	112	161	177
Kentucky	August 1	23	56	77	93
Louisiana	August 1	31	92	121	137
Maine	August 1	13	13	13	14
Maryland	September 1	62	145	298	348
Massachusetts	August 1	0	0	0	1
Michigan	October 1	36	89	184	225
Minnesota	August 1	15	29	37	49
Mississippi	August 1	19	58	71	75
Missouri	August 15	101	166	289	322
Montana	August 1	149	153	198	214
Nebraska	August 1	12	39	49	61
Nevada	August 1	56	125	147	181
New Hampshire	July 1	43	78	123	148
New Jersey	August 15	108	216	416	507
New Mexico	August 1	133	198	322	354
New York	October 1	201	411	847	1,075
North Carolina	August 1	513	674	1,106	1,302

State	Date Coverage Began (in 2010)	11/1/2010 Enrollment	2/1/2011 Enrollment	3/31/2011 Enrollment	4/30/2011 Enrollment
North Dakota	August 1	1	5	6	9
Ohio	September 1	634	726	1,024	1,145
Oklahoma	September 1	148	190	262	291
Oregon	August 1	340	483	734	822
Pennsylvania	October 1	1,657	2,046	2,684	3,191
Rhode Island	September 15	78	85	102	115
South Carolina	August 1	104	242	309	377
South Dakota	July 15	43	62	94	94
Tennessee	August 1	43	171	255	314
Texas	August 1	393	1,007	1,298	1,528
Utah	September 1	73	117	223	286
Vermont	September 1	0	0	0	0
Virginia	August 1	75	204	268	320
Washington	September 1	75	139	304	341
West Virginia	September 1	4	15	18	24
Wisconsin	August 1	248	307	456	547
Wyoming	August 1	17	49	61	73
	Totals	7,986	12,437	18,313	21,454

Sources: U.S. Department of Health and Human Services, "State by State Enrollment in the Pre-Existing Condition Insurance Plan, Archived Enrollment Data," November 1, 2010, available at http://www.healthcare.gov/news/factsheets/pcip02102011b.html; U.S. Department of Health and Human Services, State by State Enrollment in the Pre-Existing Condition Insurance Plan," February 1, 2011, available at http://www.healthcare.gov/news/ factsheets/pcip02102011a.html; and U.S. Department of Health and Human Services, "State by State Enrollment in the Pre-Existing Condition Insurance Plan," April 30, 2011, available at http://www.healthcare.gov/news/factsheets/pcip06102011a.html.

Notes: Maine, Massachusetts, New Jersey, New York, and Vermont all have laws that in varying ways guarantee issue of health insurance and prohibit insurers from denying a person coverage based upon preexisting conditions. Residents of these states will therefore not have letters of denial or riders from insurers to use in the PCIP eligibility. The federal "proof of denial" requirements (for Vermont and Massachusetts) were modified to accept documentation that shows the individual was offered coverage in the last six months at a premium at least twice as much as the PCIP premium in the state. In Maine and New York, eligibility for the state-administered PCIP is restricted to individuals with certain health conditions that are included in a list of 30 selected conditions. In New Jersey, insurers cannot deny coverage because of a preexisting condition, but can impose an exclusion period for treatment of the preexisting condition. A person is eligible for the New Jersey PCIP if he or she has a condition that a carrier would have temporarily excluded from coverage.

Plan Benefits and Premium Rates

Specific coverage policy (e.g., providers and procedures covered and prescription drug formularies) is not addressed by the law. In other words, section 1101 PPACA does not require nor expressly prohibit certain providers, procedures, prescriptions drugs, or medical technology. However, the Secretary does have the authority to establish additional requirements for the program that can be used to establish coverage policy.[44] With respect to network adequacy, the Secretary established by regulation that each PCIP may specify the network of providers it contracts with, but the PCIP must demonstrate to HHS that it has a sufficient number and range of providers to ensure that all covered services are reasonably available to enrollees.[45] The Secretary further established that PCIPs must cover certain benefit categories listed below.[46] Specific covered items and services within these broad coverage categories may vary between PCIPs. The Secretary also established the following excluded coverage categories: (1) cosmetic surgery except to restore bodily function or correct deformity resulting from disease; (2) custodial care except for hospice; (3) in vitro fertilization, artificial insemination or any other artificial means used to cause pregnancy; (4) abortion services except when the life of the woman would be endangered or when the pregnancy is the result of an act of rape or incest; and (5) experimental care except as part of an FDA-approved clinical trial.[47]

PPACA also establishes certain benefits requirements with respect to the value of the PCIP coverage. To be a qualified PCIP, the health insurance coverage must have an actuarial value of at least 65% of the total allowed costs.[48] The means that the PCIP's average share of the total the costs of the coverage benefits must be at least 65%. The coverage must also have an out-of-pocket limit no greater than the applicable amount for high-deductible health plans linked to health savings accounts, which is \$5,950 for an individual in 2011.[49] This means the total annual cost-sharing requirements, including deductibles, cannot exceed \$5,950. This limit, however, does not apply to deductibles and expenses for out-of-network services if the plan uses a network of providers.[50] There is considerable variation in cost sharing between states and PCIP options within a state. For 2011, PCIP medical deductibles range from \$0 to \$5,000 and for PCIPs with separate drug deductibles the range is \$100 to \$500.[51] After the deductible, some PCIPs have a coinsurance requirement while other PCIPs use flat dollar co-payments. For example, PCIPs that utilize coinsurance typically require around 20% for a primary care visit, while the flat dollar co-payments for the same visit in other PCIPs is typically around $20 to $25.[52]

REQUIRED PCIP BENEFIT CATEGORIES AT 45 CFR §152.19(A)

- Hospital inpatient services
- Hospital outpatient services
- Mental health and substance abuse services
- Professional services for the diagnosis or treatment of injury, illness, or condition
- Non-custodial skilled nursing services
- Home health services
- Durable medical equipment and supplies
- Diagnostic x-rays and laboratory tests
- Physical therapy services
- Hospice services
- Emergency services including ambulance services
- Prescription drugs
- Preventive care
- Maternity care

Certain PPACA requirements for the PCIP are designed to make premium rates fair and affordable. By law, premium rates for the PCIP must be established at a standard rate for a standard population and age rating cannot exceed a factor of 4 to 1.[53] PPACA also subsidizes premiums by appropriating $5 billion for the payment of claims and administrative costs of the PCIP that are in excess of the amount of premiums collected from enrollees.[54] In addition to the population and age rating factors, PCIP premiums vary considerably by state and by plan benefit factors, such as, the size of the deductible.[55] For 2011, monthly premiums for PCIPs administrated by a state range from $69 to $1,806 and for the federal PCIPs premiums range from $116 to $842.[56]

Reducing 2011 Premiums

In order to reduce the out-of-pocket premium costs that may have been high enough to discourage enrolling in the PCIPs, HHS announced on May 31, 2011, that it would be reducing premiums in the federally administered

PCIPs.[57] Effective July 2011, premiums will drop an average of 20.67%.[58] These premium decreases help bring PCIP premiums closer to the rates in each state's individual insurance market (**Table 2**). In Hawaii, Idaho, Massachusetts, North Dakota, Vermont, and Wyoming, PCIP premiums were similar to the individual market and will not be reduced.

HHS concurrently released guidance to the states on how they may reduce premiums in the state-administered PCIPs.[59] To date, it is unknown how many states plan on adjusting premiums in their PCIPs.

Table 2. July 2011 Reductions in Federally Administered PCIP Premiums

State	PCIP Premium Reduction
Alabama	-40.0%
Arizona	-40.0%
Delaware	-40.0%
District of Columbia	-18.3%
Florida	-40.0%
Georgia	-15.5%
Hawaii	No Change
Idaho	No Change
Indiana	-26.2%
Kentucky	-40.0%
Louisiana	-24.8%
Massachusetts	No Change
Minnesota	-38.3%
Mississippi	-2.1%
Nebraska	-20.5%
Nevada	-37.5%
North Dakota	No Change
South Carolina	-14.7%
Tennessee	-18.4%
Texas	-23.6%
Vermont	No Change
Virginia	-40.3%
West Virginia	-15.8%
Wyoming	No Change

Source: U.S. Department of Health and Human Services, "Changes to the Pre-Existing Condition Insurance Plan in Your State," May 31, 2011, available at http://www.healthcare.gov/news/factsheets/pcip05312011a.html.

APPENDIX. PCIP PROGRAM TABLES

Table A-1. PCIP Websites by State

State	Name	Website
Alaska	Alaska Comprehensive Health Association	http://www.achia.com/ACHIA-FED/benefits.htm
Arkansas	Federal Pre-Existing Condition Insurance Plan (PCIP)	http://www.chiparkansas.org/pcip/default.asp
California	California Pre-Existing Condition Insurance Plan (PCIP)	http://www.pcip.ca.gov/Home/default.aspx
Colorado	Getting US Covered	https://www.gettinguscovered.org/
Connecticut	Connecticut Pre-Existing Condition Insurance Plan	http://www.ct.gov/dss/cwp/view.asp?Q=463668&A=2345
Illinois	Illinois Pre-Existing Condition Insurance Plan (IPXP)	http://insurance.illinois.gov/IPXP/
Iowa	Iowa Comprehensive Health Association (HIPIOWA)	http://www.hipiowa.com/
Kansas	Pre-existing Condition Insurance Plan-Kansas (PCIP-KS)	http://www.khiastatepool.com/default.asp
Maine	Pre-Existing Condition Plan	http://www.dirigohealth.maine.gov/Pages/pre_exist.html
Maryland	Maryland Health Insurance Plan (MHIP)	http://www.marylandhealthinsuranceplan.state.md.us/
Michigan	Health Insurance Program (HIP) Michigan	http://www.hipmichigan.com/
Missouri	Missouri Health Insurance Pool (MHIP)	http://www.mhip.org/
Montana	Montana Affordable Care Plan (MAC Plan)	http://www.mthealth.org/
New Hampshire	NHHP-FED	http://www.nhhp.org/nhhp-fed/index.asp
New Jersey	NJ Protect	http://www.state.nj.us/dobi/division_insurance/njprotect/index.htm
New Mexico	New Mexico Federal High Risk Pool (FHRP)	http://www.nmmip.org/
New York	NY Bridge Plan	http://www.ins.state.ny.us/health/high_risk.htm
North Carolina	Inclusive Health - Federal Option	http://www.inclusivehealth.org/federal option/index.htm
Ohio	Ohio High Risk Pool	http://www.ohiohighriskpool.com/
Oklahoma	Oklahoma Temporary High Risk Pool	http://www.bcbsok.com/ohrp/temp_pool.html
Oregon	Oregon Federal Medical Insurance Pool (FMIP)	http://www.oregon.gov/OPHP/OMIP/fmip.shtml

Table A-1. (Continued)

State	Name	Website
Pennsylvania	PA Fair Care	http://www.pafaircare.com/
Rhode Island	Pre-existing Condition Insurance Plan for Rhode Island (PCIPRI)	https://www.bcbsri.com/BCBSRIWeb /plansandservices/PECIPRI/index.jsp
South Dakota	South Dakota Federal High Risk Pool Program	http://fedhighriskpool.sd.gov/
Utah	Federal-HIPUtah	http://selecthealth.org/plans/ government/fedhip/Pages/home.aspx
Washington	Pre-existing Condition Insurance Plan-Washington State (PCIP-WA)	https://www.wship.org/PCIP-WA/ default.htm
Wisconsin	Federal Health Insurance Risk-Sharing Plan (HIRSP)	http://www.hirsp.org/index.shtml
Federally-administered PCIP states	Pre-Existing Condition Insurance Plan	http://www.pciplan.com

Source: CRS analysis.

Note: The federally-administered PCIP states are Alabama, Arizona, Delaware, DC, Florida, Georgia, Hawaii, Idaho, Indiana, Kentucky, Louisiana, Massachusetts, Minnesota, Mississippi, Nebraska, Nevada, North Dakota, South Carolina, Tennessee, Texas, Vermont, Virginia, West Virginia, and Wyoming.

Table A-2. Proposed Allocation of Federal Funds for Temporary High Risk Pools, by State

State	Potential Allocation of Federal HRP Funds (in millions)
Alabama	$69
Alaska	$13
Arizona	$129
Arkansas	$46
California	$761
Colorado	$90
Connecticut	$50
Delaware	$13
District of Columbia	$9
Florida	$351
Georgia	$177
Hawaii	$16
Idaho	$24
Illinois	$196
Indiana	$93
Iowa	$35

State	Potential Allocation of Federal HRP Funds (in millions)
Kansas	$36
Kentucky	$63
Louisiana	$71
Maine	$17
Maryland	$85
Massachusetts	$77
Michigan	$141
Minnesota	$68
Mississippi	$47
Missouri	$81
Montana	$16
Nebraska	$23
Nevada	$61
New Hampshire	$20
New Jersey	$141
New Mexico	$37
New York	$297
North Carolina	$145
North Dakota	$8
Ohio	$152
Oklahoma	$60
Oregon	$66
Pennsylvania	$160
Rhode Island	$13
South Carolina	$74
South Dakota	$11
Tennessee	$97
Texas	$493
Utah	$40
Vermont	$8
Virginia	$113
Washington	$102
West Virginia	$27
Wisconsin	$73
Wyoming	$8
Totals	$5 billion

Sources: U.S. Department of Health and Human Services, "HHS Secretary Sebelius Announces New Pre-Existing Condition Insurance Plan," July 1, 2010, available at http://www.hhs.gov/news/press/2010pres/07/20100701a.html; U.S. Department of Health and Human Services, "Fact Sheet – Temporary HRP Program," April 2010. Available at http://www.hhs.gov/ociio/initiative/hi_risk_pool_facts.html.

End Notes

[1] Lynn Gruber, "How state health insurance pools are helping Americans," National Association of State Comprehensive Health Insurance Plans, January 6, 2009. High risk pools are often called health insurance associations or comprehensive health insurance associations. The Connecticut Health Care Act of 1975 created the first state high risk pool followed by the Minnesota Comprehensive Health Association in 1976.

[2] United States Government Accountability Office, Health Insurance: Enrollment, Benefits, Funding, and Other Characteristics of State High-Risk Health Insurance Pools, July 22, 2009.

[3] Ibid.

[4] Kaiser Family Foundation, *State High Risk Pool Programs and Enrollment*, December 2008. Available at http://www.statehealthfacts.org/comparetable.jsp?ind=602&cat=7. North Carolina established the 35th state high risk pool in 2009. For more background information on state high risk pools, see CRS Report RL31745, *Health Insurance: State High Risk Pools*, by Bernadette Fernandez.

[5] Lynn R. Gruber, "State high risk pools hold value in the era of health reform," National Association of State Comprehensive Health Insurance Plans Board of Directors, November 15, 2007. The National Association of State Comprehensive Health Insurance Plans (NASCHIP) was created in 1993 to provide educational opportunities and information for state high risk health insurance pools that have been, or are yet to be, established by state governments to serve the medically "uninsurable" population.

[6] Health plan and insurance enrollments generally are effective on a monthly basis, thus July 1, 2010, would be the actual start date for coverage.

[7] §1201 PPACA: §2704 PHSA. A preexisting condition exclusion means denying benefits for chronic illnesses or injuries, like carpal tunnel syndrome, diabetes, heart disease, and cancer, that an individual had before obtaining the current health insurance coverage.

[8] §1201 PPACA: §2702 PHSA. Some states already have guaranteed issue requirements under state law.

[9] Government Employees Health Association, Inc., "Pre-Existing Condition Insurance Plan administered by GEHA: Benefits Summary," July 2010, available at http://www.pciplan.com/forms/pdfs/BenefitsSummary.pdf.

[10] North Carolina Health Insurance Risk Pool, Inc., "Inclusive Health - Federal and State Option," 2010, available at http://www.inclusivehealth.org.

[11] §1101(b)(1) of PPACA. Eligible entities other than a state must be a non-profit organization.

[12] U.S. Department of Health and Human Services, "Statement of Organization, Functions, and Delegations of Authority," *Federal Register*, Vol. 75, No. 74 , Monday, April 19, 2010.

[13] Julie Appleby, "Appointments of federal watchdogs suggest more tough scrutiny for insurers," *Washington Post*, June 1, 2010, available at http://www.washingtonpost.com/wp-dyn/content/article/2010/05/31/AR2010053102756.html.

[14] 76 *Federal Register* 4703.

[15] CMS, "CMS Leadership, Center for Consumer Information and Insurance Oversight," March 29, 2011, available at http://www.cms.gov/CMSLeadership/36_Office_CCIIO.asp#TopOfPage.

[16] §1101(b)(2) of PPACA.

[17] U.S. Department of Health and Human Services, "Solicitation For Third Party Administrators For Federal High Risk Pool Program," May 25, 2010, available at https://www.fbo.gov/spg/HHS/PSC/DAM/10-233-SOL-00200/listing.html.

[18] U.S. Department of Health and Human Services, "Initiatives and Programs: Pre-Existing Condition Insurance Plan," July 2010, available at http://www.hhs.gov/ociio/initiative/index.html. U.S. Department of Health and Human Services, "Federal High Risk Pool Third

Party Administrator (10-233-SOL-00200): Interested Parties List," June 2010, available at https://www.fbo.gov/spg/HHS/PSC/DAM/10-233-SOL-00200/listing.html.

[19] CRS Report RS21974, *Federal Employees Health Benefits Program: Available Health Insurance Options*, by Hinda Chaikind and Mark Newsom.

[20] §1101(g)(1) of PPACA.

[21] January 8, 2010, memorandum "Estimated Financial Effects of the Patient Protection and Affordable Care Act as Passed by the Senate on December 24, 2009" from CMS Chief Actuary Richard S. Foster to the Congress. Available at http://www.cms.gov/Actuarial Studies/Downloads/S_PPACA_2010-01-08.pdf.

[22] Congressional Budget Office, "Letter to Senator Michael B. Enzi," June 21, 2010, available at http://www.cbo.gov/ftpdocs/115xx/doc11572/06-21-High-Risk_Insurance_Pools.pdf.

[23] April 30, 2010, letter from Governor Rick Perry to Secretary Kathleen Sebelius. Available at http://governor.state.tx.us/files/press-office/O-SebeliusKathleen20100430.pdf.

[24] Leigh Anne G. Manlove, "Governor Freudenthal Opts for Federally Run High-Risk Insurance Pool," April 28, 2010. Available at http://governor.wy.gov/press-releases/governor-freudenthal-opts-for-federally-run-highrisk-insurance-pool.html.

[25] §1101(g)(2) of PPACA.

[26] U.S. Department of Health and Human Services, "Fact Sheet – Temporary High Risk Pool Program," April 2010.Available at http://www.hhs.gov/ociio/initiative/hi_risk_pool_facts.html.

[27] §1101(d) of PPACA.

[28] 45 CFR 146.113 defines a public health plan as any plan established or maintained by a state, the U.S. government, a foreign country, or any political subdivision of a state, the U.S. government, or a foreign country that provides health coverage to individuals who are enrolled in the plan.

[29] U.S. Department of Health and Human Services, "Pre-Existing Condition Insurance Plan Eligibility and Access to Other Creditable Coverage (Policy Letter #5)," March 23, 2011.

[30] §1101(d) of PPACA.

[31] 75 *Federal Register* 45014-45033.

[32] §1101(d) of PPACA.

[33] U.S. Department of Health and Human Services, "Notice of Computer Matching Program, SSA With the United States Department of Agriculture (USDA), National Finance Center (NFC)," *Federal Register*, P.40770, vol. 75, no.134, Wednesday, July 14, 2010.

[34] See http://www.pcip.gov/Apply.html.

[35] U.S. Department of Health and Human Services, "Instructions for Completing Your Application for the Pre-Existing Condition Insurance Plan," June 2010, available at http://www.pcip.gov/PreExistingConditionPlan_EnrollmentForm_063010_508.pdf.

[36] State contact information is available at http://www.pcip.gov/StatePlans.html.

[37] U.S. Department of Health and Human Services, "Pre-Existing Condition Insurance Plan State Information," available at http://www.pcip.gov/StatePlans.html.

[38] Congressional Budget Office, "Letter to Senator Michael B. Enzi," June 21, 2010, available at http://www.cbo.gov/ftpdocs/115xx/doc11572/06-21-High-Risk_Insurance_Pools.pdf.

[39] Ibid.

[40] Centers for Medicare & Medicaid Services, "FY 2012 Online Performance Appendix," February 2011.

[41] Testimony of OCIIO Director Steven Larsen, in U.S. Congress, House Committee on Energy and Commerce, Subcommittee on Oversight and Investigations, "The PPACA's High Risk Pool Regime: High Cost, Low Participation," 112th Congress, 1st session, April 1, 2011.

[42] U.S. Department of Health and Human Services, "Changes to the Pre-Existing Condition Insurance Plan in Your State," May 31, 2011, available at http://www.healthcare.gov/news/factsheets/pcip05312011a.html.

[43] Applicants will still need to meet other eligibility criteria, including that they are U.S. citizens or residing in the United States legally and that they have been without health coverage for six months.

[44] §1101(c)(2)(D) of PPACA.

[45] 45 CFR §152.22.

[46] 45 CFR §152.19(a).

[47] 45 CFR §152.19(b).

[48] §1101(c)(2)(B) of PPACA. The actuarial value of a health insurance policy is the percentage of the total covered expenses that the plan would, on average, cover. For example, a plan with a 65% actuarial value means that consumers would on average pay 35% of the cost of health care expenses through features like deductibles and coinsurance. The amount that individual consumers pay could vary substantially by the amount of services used. The actuarial value does not include premiums paid by the enrollee.

[49] §1101(c)(2)(B) of PPACA and §223(c)(2) of the Internal Revenue Code of 1986.

[50] Department of the Treasury, Internal Revenue Service, "Health Savings Accounts and Other Tax-Favored Health Plans," Publication 969, November 25, 2009.

[51] Richard Popper, "Immediate Improvements in the Insurance Market for Americans over 50 The Early Retiree Reinsurance Program and the Pre-existing Condition Insurance Plan," presentation before the Alliance for Health Reform, January 24, 2011.

[52] CRS analysis of PCIP benefit packages.

[53] §1101(c)(2)(C) of PPACA. The terms "standard rate" and "standard population" were not defined by PPACA. HHS has interpreted this provisions to mean that the rate may not exceed 100% of the standard non-group rate. U.S. Department of Health and Human Services, "Fact Sheet—Temporary High Risk Pool Program," April 2010. Available at http://www.hhs.gov/ociio/initiative/hi_risk_pool_facts.html. Age rating refers to the practice of a health insurer estimating the expected health care spending for all individuals within a given age group and then varying the premiums for individuals across groups to account for the differences. Higher age groups are charged higher premiums.

[54] §1101(g) of PPACA.

[55] For a background in factors that impact on premium rates, see CRS Report R41588, *Private Health Insurance Premiums and Rate Reviews*, by Mark Newsom and Bernadette Fernandez.

[56] Richard Popper, "Immediate Improvements in the Insurance Market for Americans over 50 The Early Retiree Reinsurance Program and the Pre-existing Condition Insurance Plan," presentation before the Alliance for Health Reform, January 24, 2011.

[57] U.S. Department of Health and Human Services, "HHS to Reduce Premiums, Make it Easier for Americans with Pre-Existing Conditions to Get Health Insurance," May 31, 2011, available at http://www.hhs.gov/news/press/2011pres/05/ 20110531b.html.

[58] U.S. Department of Health and Human Services, "Changes to the Pre-Existing Condition Insurance Plan in Your State," May 31, 2011, available at http://www.healthcare.gov/news/ factsheets/pcip05312011a.html.

[59] U.S. Department of Health and Human Services, "PCIP Premium and Benefit Revisions (Policy Letter #6)," May 31, 2011.

In: High Risk Health Insurance Pools
Editor: Jenny Alvarez

ISBN: 978-1-62417-421-6

Chapter 2

STATEMENT OF STEVEN B. LARSEN, DEPUTY ADMINISTRATOR AND DIRECTOR, CENTER FOR CONSUMER INFORMATION AND INSURANCE OVERSIGHT, CENTERS FOR MEDICARE AND MEDICAID SERVICES. HEARING ON "THE PPACA'S HIGH RISK POOL REGIME: HIGH COST LOW PARTICIPATION"*

Chairman Stearns, Ranking Member DeGette, and Members of the Subcommittee, thank you for the opportunity to discuss the Department of Health and Human Services' work implementing the Affordable Care Act. I serve as Deputy Administrator and Director of the Center for Consumer Information & Insurance Oversight (CCIIO) within the Centers for Medicare & Medicaid Services (CMS). Since taking on this role, I have been involved in CCIIO's implementation of many of the provisions of the Affordable Care Act, including overseeing private health insurance reforms, assisting States to

* This is an edited, reformatted and augmented version of the testimony given on April 1, 2011 before the House Committee on Energy and Commerce, Subcommittee on Oversight and Investigations.

implement Health Insurance Exchanges (Exchanges), and ensuring that consumers have access to information about their rights and coverage options. Prior to becoming the Director of CCIIO, I served as the Director of the Office of Oversight within CCIIO, which is charged with working with the States to ensure compliance with the new insurance market rules, such as the prohibitions on pre-existing condition exclusions for children and rescissions, as well as ensuring consumer value for premium payments through the medical loss ratio standards and the review of unreasonable rate increases as well as the enforcement of the new restrictions on annual dollar limits on benefits.

As a former State Insurance Commissioner, I understand the key role that States play in the regulation of insurance and insurance markets. I have seen first-hand the importance of holding insurance companies accountable, and understand the need to make quality, affordable coverage more accessible to all health care consumers. I have also served as an executive in a for-profit, publicly-traded managed care company, and understand the need for competitive and robust markets as well as reasonable regulations. The Affordable Care Act appropriately balances these objectives.

At this time last year, Congress passed and the President signed into law the Affordable Care Act, which expands access to affordable, quality coverage to over 30 million Americans and strengthens consumer protections to ensure individuals have coverage when they need it most. Immediate reforms include a critical foundation of patients' rights in the private health insurance market that help put Americans in charge of their own health care. Over the past year, we have already implemented historic private market reforms including eliminating pre-existing condition exclusions for children, prohibiting insurance companies from rescinding coverage absent fraud or intentional misrepresentation of material fact and from imposing lifetime dollar limits on coverage, and enabling many dependent young adult children to stay on their parent's insurance plan up to age 26. These changes have empowered consumers and eliminated some of the worst insurance industry practices. We have heard from many people across the country that these new rights and protections are providing them with the assistance they need to keep their coverage, see the doctors of their choice, and choose the careers that best suit their talents.

Development of the Pre-Existing Condition Insurance Plan (PCIP)

The PCIP program is based on existing high-risk pools which have a history of bipartisan support. Established under section 1101 of the Affordable Care Act, the PCIP program provides a lifeline to uninsured Americans who private insurers have either refused to insure because of a pre-existing condition or have offered coverage that excludes benefits associated with that condition. These Americans can now receive health coverage without limitation on benefits because of their condition. The PCIP program provides a critical bridge from the existing insurance market to the new patient-centered insurance system that will come into effect with the Health Insurance Exchanges in 2014.

I'm proud of the fact that the States and the Federal government have been able to stand up programs in every State in record time. We are working with the States and our partners in the patient advocacy community to increase public awareness of this important bridge program. Already, thousands of Americans who were locked out of accessible private insurance coverage before the passage of the law have this valuable and needed coverage. For example, the PCIP program has provided invaluable help to people like Jerry Garner. Mr. Garner, a real estate agent from Gowen, Michigan who was recently featured in the *New York Times*, lost his health insurance after undergoing a kidney transplant. Because of his pre-existing condition, he was unable to obtain new insurance to cover the $2,000 monthly drug bills for the immunosuppressive medications that transplant patients must take to prevent rejection of a new organ. Mr. Garner signed up for Michigan's PCIP program and is now paying lower premiums than he did under his previous insurance and is receiving more comprehensive coverage. Mr. Garner's wife told the *New York Times* that the PCIP program "was definitely an answered prayer."[1]

I'm pleased that enrollment in PCIP programs has increased by 50 percent from our November release to our February release of enrollment data, and we expect it to continue to grow between now and 2014. As we implement this benefit, CCIIO is actively working with States, consumer groups, patient advocates, voluntary health organizations, health care providers, social workers, other Federal agencies, and the insurance industry to promote the program, including holding meetings with State officials, consumer groups, and others. The remainder of my testimony will discuss the details of this significant new program.

By statute, the PCIP program is specifically targeted to U.S. citizens and people who reside in the U.S. legally who have been denied coverage because of a pre-existing condition and have been without coverage for at least 6 months. PCIP is intended to be a bridge program to provide uninsured people with a pre-existing condition access to comprehensive coverage between now and 2014. In 2014, most insurers will no longer be able to discriminate based on pre-existing conditions, and individuals and small businesses will have access to more affordable and robust private insurance choices through new competitive Exchanges. Until then, uninsured people who have been denied care or charged more because of a pre-existing condition – such as cancer, diabetes, high blood pressure, or high cholesterol – now have a chance for more affordable coverage where they may never have had one before. A March 2011 report from the Government Accountability Office (GAO) noted that insurance application denial rates varied significantly across insurance issuers, with a quarter of issuers having denial rates of 15 percent or less and another quarter having denial rates of 40 percent or more.[2]

The PCIP program was required to be operational within 90 days of enactment of the Affordable Care Act, and CCIIO worked with States to meet that aggressive deadline. The Affordable Care Act appropriated $5 billion for the PCIP program, and allows States the choice of administering their own PCIP program or, in a State that declines to do so, having CCIIO administer the program. To implement the Federally-administered PCIP program, CCIIO partnered with the Office of Personnel Management (OPM) to issue a competitive solicitation to entities that provide health insurance coverage on a national level, including Federal Employees Health Benefits (FEHB) plan carriers. CCIIO proceeded to contract with the Government Employees Health Association (GEHA) to serve as the third-party administrator for the Federal PCIP program, with OPM managing the contract for CCIIO. In addition, the U.S. Department of Agriculture's National Finance Center performs eligibility and enrollment processing.

In April 2010, we proposed an allocation of PCIP funding among the States, based on the formula used for distributing funds in the Children's Health Insurance Program (CHIP). In July 2010, we issued an interim final rule with a 60-day comment period which outlined the design of the program and solicited input from stakeholders.[3] Twenty-seven States are now administering their own PCIP program, while twenty-three States and the District of Columbia instead chose the Federal government to administer their State PCIP programs. CCIIO has also issued five guidance documents since the regulation's publication, which explain: general compliance requirements for Federal PCIP contractors; how newborns are covered under a PCIP program; how portability of coverage and third party payments work under the PCIP program; how a child under the age of 19 may qualify for the Federally-administered PCIP program; and that a PCIP program may not deny coverage to an otherwise qualified individual eligible for other coverage.

ENROLLMENT

Individuals can apply to the PCIP program that serves their State by completing an application and providing the supporting documentation that the PCIP program requires to establish eligibility. Once enrolled, applicants have access to a wide array of benefit designs in the States, including plans that are compatible with health savings accounts, and tools designed to improve health such as a health risk assessment and care management. In some States, enrollees in the PCIP program who take the health risk assessment qualify for a financial incentive. While enrollees are given a choice of benefit designs, all 2011 plan options provide the following: first-dollar preventive care; no lifetime maximum benefits; no waiting periods; coverage for all major medical services; and an annual out-of-pocket limit on spending.

The PCIP program is designed to meet the needs of beneficiaries with pre-existing conditions and provide coverage for people with significant medical expenses and few available coverage options until 2014. According to enrollment data reported as of February 1, 2011, a total of 12,437 individuals have been enrolled in PCIP programs across the country. Of this total, 8,762 people have been enrolled in State-run PCIPs in 27 States and 3,675 have been enrolled in Federally-administered PCIPs in 23 States and the District of Columbia. In addition to the payment of medical and other claims, spending has included one-time program design and development costs, as well as enrollment, eligibility processing, billing, premium collection and consumer support functions including an online web application and call center to help facilitate enrollment.

PARTNERSHIPS WITH STATES

In implementing the PCIP program, we worked closely with our State partners to ensure they were able to appropriately tailor their State-administered PCIP programs to their local insurance markets. The PCIP program was modeled after the high-risk pool programs that exist in many States to assist individuals who could not obtain coverage in the private market and were ineligible for such public programs as Medicare and Medicaid. The PCIP program also draws many features from the popular bipartisan CHIP program – covering a broad range of health benefits, including those for pre-existing conditions, and allowing for significant State flexibility in design and details. The program ensures maximum efficiency in distribution of funding by permitting individual States to determine when to draw down their allocated funds. If necessary, unused State allocations could be redistributed to other States that have consumers in need.

We are closely monitoring Federal and State expenditures to ensure that States appropriately manage their funding and do not exhaust their allocations prematurely. Each State contract includes an early warning or trigger provision; when a State has reached 75 percent of its projected enrollment or expenditures are on track to exceed a State's allotment, the State must consult with CCIIO to ensure plans are in place to manage the remainder of their allocation appropriately. Similar to CHIP, administrative expenses in the PCIP program are limited by a 10 percent cap for the duration of the program. CCIIO and States work together closely to monitor expenditures to ensure we are maximizing the value of the program while staying within the 10 percent administrative cost limit and within the total funds allocated.

The flexibility for States that is a hallmark of the PCIP program means that no two State-administered programs are identical. PCIP programs are uniquely tailored to the insurance market conditions in each State. For example, some States have chosen to build their PCIP programs off of their existing high risk pools, while others chose to establish a new pool. Additionally, because each State insurance market is different, premiums vary among the different States. It also means that, together with the States, we have had the opportunity to improve the affordability of coverage and to enhance our outreach efforts. For example, we recently adjusted the Federal PCIP program to reduce premiums by approximately 20 percent, and added two new plan choices which improve benefit design for all current enrollees and new applicants. States such as North Carolina have also reduced premiums in 2011. In this State, since January 1, 2011, premiums for people up to age 55 declined by about 10 percent, while premiums declined as much as 31 percent for people above age 55.

Outreach Efforts

CCIIO has an aggressive strategy to encourage enrollment of eligible individuals, meeting with local doctors, hospitals, consumer groups and chapters of advocacy groups like the American Cancer Society and American Diabetes Association. For example, we are working to reach local stakeholders and providers who come into contact with people with chronic care needs in need of insurance to spread awareness about the PCIP program. We have actively reached out to provider groups through webinars, arranged meetings with potential partners in at least six States, and will continue this outreach in the coming months. CMS is also working with agencies that have a history serving individuals with disabilities, such as the Social Security Administration. Since February 15, 2011, all applicants for Social Security disability benefits have been informed about the PCIP program through application receipts. These collaborations leverage existing communication channels with individuals who have a pre-existing condition and may therefore be eligible for the PCIP program.

I am pleased to report that enrollment has grown significantly over the past several months and we anticipate continued growth. We believe that PCIP programs administered by the States and the Federal government will continue to fill a market void and provide valuable health insurance coverage to a population that desperately needs it until 2014. In 2014, State-based Health Insurance Exchanges will provide affordable, quality health insurance coverage to any American who needs it. We believe that the PCIP program is a vital bridge to 2014 which provides comprehensive coverage to vulnerable individuals and their families, and we look forward to continuing to improve the program.

Moving Forward

As we lay the groundwork for 2014, it is our intention to continue implementing vital consumer protections while offering enough flexibility to ensure that the market is not disrupted. We are proud of all that we have accomplished over the past year and look forward to 2014 when Americans will have access to more affordable, comprehensive health insurance plans. With the new coverage options available in the PCIP program, uninsured individuals with pre-existing conditions no longer need to wait and worry that their illness will bankrupt them, or that they will have to choose between a roof over their head and paying for the cancer treatment they so desperately need. The PCIP program is another important program that will lead our transition to the new era of health insurance coverage for all Americans, through the Exchanges, in 2014.

In the meantime, I look forward to continuing to work on implementing provisions of the Affordable Care Act, strengthening CCIIO's partnership with Congress, the States, consumers, and other stakeholders across the country. Thank you for the opportunity to discuss the work that CCIIO has been doing to implement the Affordable Care Act.

End Notes

[1] Walecia Konrad, "Pre-existing Condition? Now, a Health Policy May Not Be Impossible." The *New York Times*, March 18, 2011, link here.

[2] GAO Report, *Private Health Insurance: Data on Application and Coverage Denials*, GAO-11-268 (Mar. 2011).

[3] Pre-Existing Conditions Insurance Plan Program, 75 Fed. Reg. 45014 (July 30, 2010).

In: High Risk Health Insurance Pools
Editor: Jenny Alvarez
ISBN: 978-1-62417-421-6

Chapter 3

HEALTH INSURANCE: STATE HIGH RISK POOLS*

Bernadette Fernandez

SUMMARY

In an effort to expand the options for health coverage, 35 states have established high risk health insurance pools. These programs target individuals who cannot obtain or afford health insurance in the private market, primarily because of preexisting health conditions. Also, many states use their high risk pools to comply with the portability and guaranteed availability provisions of the Health Insurance Portability and Accountability Act of 1996 (P.L. 104-191).

In general, state high risk pools tend to enroll a small percentage of the uninsured. In December 2009, approximately 208,000 individuals were enrolled in high risk pools. State-established nonprofit organizations typically run these pools, with private insurance companies handling day-to-day operations, along with plan administrative staff. Although benefit packages vary across states and plans, they generally reflect health benefits that are available in the private insurance market. The majority of high risk pools cap

---

* This is an edited, reformatted and augmented version of the Congressional Research Service Publication, CRS Report for Congress RL31745, dated January 26, 2011.

premiums between 150% to 200% of market rates, and pools are subsidized through insurer assessments and other funding mechanisms.

The Trade Act of 2002 (P.L. 107-210) appropriated a total of $100 million for FY2003-FY2004. With the expiration of authorizing legislation for federal funding of state pools, the 109th Congress took up this issue. The House passed H.R. 4519, the State High Risk Pool Funding Extension Act of 2006, which reauthorized federal grants to state high risk pools through FY2010, and changed the funding formula used for such grants. The Act authorized $15 million for seed grants and $75 million for operational and bonus grants for FY2006. The Senate passed H.R. 4519 without amendment, and it was signed into law (P.L. 109-172) on February 10, 2006.

As part of the budget reconciliation process, the Senate passed S. 1932, the Deficit Reduction Act of 2005 (DRA) conference agreement, which provided appropriations for the grants authorized under H.R. 4519. The measure also included conforming language on enactment of H.R. 4519. The House agreed to the Senate-amended DRA bill, and it was signed it into law (P.L. 109-171) on February 8, 2006. The Centers for Medicare and Medicaid Services (CMS) awarded grants to 31 states that experienced operational losses in 2005. Of those 31 states, 25 also received bonus grants. In 2006, CMS awarded seed grants to five states, and to another five states in 2007.

The 110th Congress took up the issue of extending the federal grant program by making funding available pursuant to the Consolidated Appropriations Act of 2008 (P.L. 110-161). The grant funding totaled $49,127,000. In July 2008, CMS announced that 30 states received operational and bonus grants totaling $49,126,500.

The 111th Congress provided $75,000,000 in appropriations for grants to state high risk pools under the Omnibus Appropriations Act of 2009 (P.L. 111-8). On September 30, 2009, CMS awarded operational grants to 31 states and bonus grants to 28 states. Furthermore, the Consolidated Appropriations Act of 2010 (P.L. 111-117) provided $55,000,000 in additional appropriations for high risk pools.

In addition to state-established high risk pools, the Patient Protection and Affordable Care Act (PPACA, P.L. 111-148), as amended, requires the Secretary of Health and Human Services to establish a temporary high risk pool program to provide health insurance coverage for certain uninsured individuals with preexisting health conditions.

Introduction

In an effort to expand the options for health coverage, 35 states have established high risk health insurance pools.[1] These programs target individuals who cannot obtain or afford health insurance in the private market, primarily due to preexisting health conditions. High risk pools (HRPs) generally cover people who have sought health coverage in the individual (nongroup) market, but have been denied coverage, received quotes from insurers that are higher than the premiums offered by the high risk pools, or received offers from insurers that permanently exclude coverage of preexisting health conditions.[2]

Many states also use their high risk pools to comply with the portability and guaranteed availability provisions of the Health Insurance Portability and Accountability Act of 1996 (HIPAA, P.L. 104-191). For eligible individuals moving from the group to nongroup market, HIPAA requires state-licensed health insurers to make coverage available to such individuals, and prohibits exclusion of coverage for preexisting conditions. To enforce these rules, states are given a choice. They may either enforce the HIPAA individual market guarantees ("federal fallback"), or establish an "acceptable alternative state mechanism," such as a high risk health insurance pool.[3]

In general, state high risk pools tend to enroll a small percentage of the uninsured. For example, approximately 200,000 individuals were enrolled in the 34 high risk pools in operation in 2008.[4] In contrast, the Government Accountability Office (GAO) estimated that nearly 4 million additional persons were potentially eligible for enrollment.[5] However, such limited enrollment reflects, in part, the narrow focus of these pools: individuals with preexisting health conditions, who do not have access to public or group health insurance, and seek coverage in the private, non-group market.

In addition to state-established high risk pools, the 111th Congress passed the Patient Protection and Affordable Care Act (PPACA), which President Obama signed into law (P.L. 111-148) on March 23, 2010. PPACA, as amended, requires the Secretary of Health and Human Services to establish a temporary high risk pool program, prior to 2014, to provide health insurance coverage to certain individuals with preexisting health conditions who have been uninsured for six or more months.[6] This chapter will focus on the original, state-established high risk pools.

Health Insurance Context

High risk pools fill a niche in the health insurance system—a patchwork system of private markets and public programs designed to meet the needs of different types of health care consumers.[7] In the private health insurance market, most people get health coverage through the group market. This market provides health benefits to groups of people that are drawn together by an employer or other organization, such as a trade union. Such groups are generally formed for some purpose other than obtaining insurance, like employment.

While most Americans receive their health coverage through the workplace—as a current employee, a dependent of an employee, or a retiree—some individuals do not have access to employer-sponsored insurance (ESI). They may be workers who do not qualify for an offer of health benefits from their employer (e.g., because the workers have part-time or seasonal employment status), or they may work for a company that does not provide health insurance at all, or they may be unemployed. Public programs also are a source of health coverage, but individuals and families must meet eligibility requirements in order to qualify for benefits. Individuals who cannot access ESI and are not eligible for public programs may seek health insurance in the nongroup (individual) market.

Applicants to the individual insurance market must go through robust medical underwriting—the process by which an insurer considers information about an applicant and determines (1) whether to offer an insurance policy in the first place, and (2) the terms of that policy (e.g., the monthly premium). The information that a health insurer considers may include personal characteristics, such as an individual's health conditions, family medical history, and other relevant factors. Though uncommon, the insurance carrier may ask an applicant to undergo a physical exam, or provide medical specimens. In the group market, insurers forgo underwriting in the traditional sense, that is, reviewing *each* person's demographics and medical history. Instead, an insurer would consider the overall characteristics of the group, and calculate a premium for a set of benefits that would be charged to each person in the group, regardless of their individual health status. (For very small groups, insurers may individually underwrite policies, if permitted by law.)

Federal and state laws restrict somewhat insurers' ability to reject applications or design coverage based on health factors in the nongroup market. Nonetheless, some applicants are rejected from the individual market altogether, others may receive insurance offers with riders that exclude coverage for a specific health condition or body part, or others may be charged premiums that are higher than those in the group market for similar coverage.[8] Rigorous underwriting results in an enrollee population in the individual market that is fairly healthy (three out of four enrollees report that their health is excellent or very good[9]), thereby excluding persons with moderate to severe health conditions from this private market. High risk pools were designed to assist such individuals who—because of their health conditions—have very few options for private health coverage.

Health Policy Context

High risk pools appeal to policymakers who prefer an incremental approach to coverage expansion and reliance on current state oversight of health insurance.[10] Supporters of HRPs contend that states can use their existing regulatory infrastructure, as well as their knowledge of health care markets, to efficiently insure previously uninsurable individuals. Supporters also contend that the private, nongroup market will benefit. They reason that by removing high risk persons from the individual market and placing them in publicly subsidized insurance pools, coverage in the individual market will become more affordable. They argue that better risk spreading helps to stabilize the market, promote competition, and retain insurance carriers—earning the support of such organizations.[11] Moreover, HRPs function as a safety net for the nongroup market by assuring that individuals have access to health insurance as long as they are able and willing to pay for it.

Others contend that high risk pools are generally too small and underfunded to meet the needs of the majority of persons who cannot access health insurance in the private market. By design, HRPs experience losses, but federal attempts to subsidize these losses have been limited. Premiums combined with other cost-sharing requirements can often make the coverage offered by these pools unaffordable. Moreover, most state HRPs exclude coverage for preexisting conditions for six months or more.[12] As a result, some researchers remain skeptical that high risk pools will be able to substantially reduce the number of uninsured, particularly among those with serious medical conditions.[13] With respect to reducing the number of people without health coverage, consumer groups generally advocate for expansion of the federal role in providing coverage, whether through existing public programs or broader health care reform,[14] not unlike some of the private market reforms included under PPACA.

While state high risk pools have existed since the mid-1970s, congressional support of state pools began in the 1990s. The enactment of HIPAA during the 104th Congress specified state HRPs as acceptable mechanisms for complying with the group-to-individual market requirements. The 107th Congress passed the Trade Act of 2002 (P.L. 107-210), which authorized a new federal program to provide grants to state high risk pools and made appropriations for FY2003 and FY2004. With expiration of the authorizing legislation for the grant program to states, the 109th Congress reauthorized the program through FY2010 and made appropriations for FY2006. The 110th Congress passed legislation in December 2007 and the 111th Congress passed legislation in March and December 2009 to provide additional appropriations to state high risk pools. (See detailed discussion under "Federal Grants to State High Risk Pools" section.)

State High Risk Pools

Currently, 35 states have high risk health insurance pools. States have a great deal of discretion regarding the establishment and operation of these pools, including covered benefits, eligibility requirements, pre-existing condition exclusion periods, and funding sources.

General Characteristics of State High Risk Pools

Administration

State high risk pools usually are operated through state-established nonprofit organizations. While private insurance companies typically are responsible for daily administrative duties (along with pool administrative staff), traditional high risk pools bear the insurance risk.[15] Boards oversee the governance of HRPs and usually consist of representatives from insurance companies, consumer groups, health care providers, and state agencies.

Premiums and Funding

In order to limit health insurance premiums for persons with costly medical conditions, all states cap high risk pool premiums (most are specified in statute). Almost all states have caps between 150% and 200% of standard risk rates. High risk pools generally operate at a loss, "because it isn't feasible to pool a group of individuals known to have major health problems and expect their premium contributions to cover the entire cost."[16] Thus, many state pools tap other sources of funding to cover their operating expenses.

States may augment premium collection with one or more of the following sources: assessments on insurers, in some instances combined with offsetting tax credits; general revenue; and other state sources.[17] Almost all states with HRPs assess a fee on insurance carriers and health maintenance organizations; two states place an assessment on hospitals.[18] Many state HRPs also receive grants from the federal government (see discussion under "Federal Grants to State High Risk Pools").

Benefits

Although health benefits provided through high risk pools vary across plans and states, they generally reflect coverage that is available in the private nongroup market. State pools usually offer more than one plan from which enrollees may choose. Deductibles and other cost-sharing requirements vary from state to state. Nearly all state HRPs have at least one plan with *lifetime* maximums on benefits (based on a dollar limit), except for Indiana and New Mexico.[19] In contrast, most pools do *not* apply *annual* maximums on benefits, except for California, Louisiana, Tennessee, Utah, and West Virginia.[20] In addition, most state HRPs exclude coverage for preexisting health conditions for 6-12 months.[21]

Eligibility

States establish the eligibility criteria for high risk pools. As noted, many states allow HIPAA-eligible persons to enroll in their HRPs. HIPAA eligibles are persons who did not have or are losing coverage and seeking it in the individual market.[22] They must meet the following requirements: (1) have at least 18 months of "creditable coverage" (specified in statute) without a significant break in that coverage (63 or more days); (2) most recent coverage must have been through a group health plan; (3) exhausted federal or state continuation coverage; (4) not eligible for Medicaid or Medicare; and (5) not have any other health insurance. For HIPAA eligibles, high risk pools guarantee the availability of health insurance and prohibit exclusion of coverage for preexisting conditions. High risk pools also are designed to address the insurance needs of non-HIPAA-eligible persons with costly medical conditions. A number of states provide for presumptive eligibility, allowing individuals to become automatically eligible for HRPs if they have a certain medical condition specified under state law. In addition to HIPAA eligibles and persons with specific conditions, many states allow individuals who have experienced coverage denials, coverage restrictions, or premium increases to enroll in high risk pools. Lastly, some states allow persons who receive the Health Coverage Tax Credit to enroll in their high risk pools.[23]

Enrollment

High risk pool participation varies significantly across states, with average enrollment ranging from a high of 27,187 participants in Minnesota to a low of 265 enrollees in Florida in December 2009. Among state HRPs, the enrollment distribution clusters toward the low end. To illustrate, two-thirds of state pools had participation below 4,000 individuals (23 states). In contrast, only seven states had more than 10,000 participants.[24]

FEDERAL GRANTS TO STATE HIGH RISK POOLS

Given that state high risk pools typically operate at a loss (see discussion above), the federal government has provided financial assistance to states during the past several years. Congress established a grant program, administered by the Centers for Medicare and Medicaid Services (CMS), to provide seed grants to states that did not already have high risk pools but wanted to establish them, and operational and bonus grants to existing state pools. Once Congress appropriates funding for these grants, CMS announces the funding opportunity and collects and reviews applications. A state may receive up to $1 million in seed grant funding; operational grant amounts are determined by formula. (Not all states with existing HRPs receive grants.)[25]

107th Congress

With enactment of the Trade Act of 2002 (P.L. 107-210), the federal government provided funding to state high risk pools for the first time. The Trade Act authorized and appropriated $20 million in the form of seed grants. Each qualifying state could receive up to $1 million to support the creation and implementation of a high risk pool. In 2003, CMS awarded seed grants to six states: Maryland ($1 million), New Hampshire ($1 million), Ohio ($150,000), South Dakota ($1 million), Utah ($52,618), and West Virginia ($1 million).[26]

The Trade Act also authorized and appropriated $80 million to be split evenly over FY2003 and FY2004 to defray some of the operating losses experienced by states with existing high risk pools. Each operational grant could cover up to 50% of a pool's operating losses for the year. To qualify, each state must have established a high risk pool that restricts premiums to no more than 150% of the premium for standard risk rates in the state, offers a choice of two or more coverage options, and has in effect a mechanism designed to ensure continued funding of losses incurred after the end of FY2004. However, states may still be able to determine, within federal standards, how much to charge enrollees in out-of-pocket costs, what benefits to include under the plans, how long coverage for preexisting conditions may be excluded, and whom among otherwise uninsurable individuals will be eligible.

Table 1 shows which states received operational grants for FY2003 and FY2004, and the funding levels. Nineteen states were awarded operational grants in FY2003; 22 states in FY2004.[27]

109th Congress

With expiration of authorizing legislation for the grant program, the House passed H.R. 4519, the State High Risk Pool Funding Extension Act of 2006, on December 17, 2005. H.R. 4519 reauthorized federal grants to state high risk pools through FY2010, and changed the funding formula used for such grants. The formula for operational grants was changed to the following: 40% to all qualifying states in equal amounts, 30% based on state proportion of uninsured population among all qualifying states, and 30% based on state proportion of the high risk pool population. H.R. 4519 also allowed operational grants to cover up to 100% of pool losses and authorized the following amounts for FY2006: $15 million for seed grants and $75 million for operational and bonus grants. The Senate passed H.R. 4519 without amendment on February 1, 2006, and President Bush signed it into law (P.L. 109-172) on February 10, 2006.

As part of the budget reconciliation process, the Senate passed S. 1932, the Deficit Reduction Act of 2005 (DRA) conference agreement. DRA included provisions that would provide specific appropriations for the grants authorized under H.R. 4519. Section 6202 of the Senate measure amended the Public Health Service Act to provide $90 million in appropriations for grants to states for FY2006. DRA provided $75 million for operational grants and $15 million for seed grants. The grants are distributed according to existing statutory requirements. This measure also included conforming language on enactment of H.R. 4519. Pursuant to H.Res. 653, the House agreed to the Senate-amended bill on February 1, 2006. On February 8, 2006, President Bush signed DRA into law (P.L. 109-171).

Table 1. Operational Grants Awarded to State High Risk Pools, FY2003 and FY2004

State	Grant amount, FY2003 ($ thousands)	Grant amount, FY2004 ($ thousands)
Alabama	2,826	—
Alaska	542	484
Arkansas	1,928	1,893
Colorado	3,219	3,096
Connecticut	1,597	1,503
Illinois	8,144	7,473
Indiana	3,266	3,358
Iowa	1,107	368
Kansas	1,462	1,297
Kentucky	2,511	2,292
Maryland	—	3,176
Massachusetts	—	132
Minnesota	1,984	1,972
Mississippi	2,066	2,038
Montana	698	621
Nebraska	894	751
New Hampshire	225	532
New Mexico	2,048	1,739
North Dakota	329	293
Oklahoma	2,931	2,731
Utah	—	1,395
Wisconsin	2,222	2,501
Wyoming	—	358

Sources: Centers for Medicare and Medicaid Services, "HHS Awards Grants to Twenty-two States to Offset Costs of Insurance for Residents Too Sick for Conventional Coverage," News Release, October 5, 2005; and K. Pollitz and E. Bangit, "Federal Aid to State High-Risk Pools: Promoting Health Insurance Coverage or Providing Fiscal Relief?" Issue Brief, November 2005.

Note: Grant amounts are rounded to the nearest thousand.

The appropriations provided under DRA were used to extend federal funding for this program. On September 30, 2006, CMS awarded seed grants to five states that wanted either to establish high risk pools or conduct feasibility studies: California ($150,000), New York ($150,000), North Carolina ($150,000), Tennessee ($1 million), and Vermont ($1 million). That same year, CMS awarded grants to 31 states that experienced operational losses in 2005. Of those 31 states, 25 also received bonus grants, exhausting the entire appropriations for operational and bonus grants. **Table 2** shows which states received operational and bonus grants.

Because the funding for seed grants was not exhausted with the 2006 awards, CMS awarded five seed grants in 2007. The states that received these grants were the District of Columbia ($150,000), Florida ($150,000), Georgia ($150,000), North Carolina ($850,000), and Rhode Island ($150,000).

110th Congress

Pursuant to the Consolidated Appropriations Act of 2008 (P.L. 110-161), Congress made additional funding available for grants to state high risk pools. CMS issued a grant notification letter to states on May 1, 2008. It stated that a total of $49,127,000 would be split to fund operational grants (two-thirds of the appropriated amount) and bonus grants (remaining one-third).[28] Applications were due by June 9, 2008.

On July 21, 2008, CMS announced that 30 states received grants totaling $49, 126,500. **Table 3** shows which states received grants and the combined grant amounts.

111th Congress

The Omnibus Appropriations Act of 2009 (P.L. 111-8) provided $75,000,000 for grants to state high risk pools. CMS announced the availability of these grants in May 2009. On September 30, 2009, CMS awarded operational grants to 31 states and bonus grants to 28 states (see **Table 4**).[29] Furthermore, the Consolidated Appropriations Act of 2010 (P.L. 111-117) provided $55,000,000 in additional appropriations for high risk pools.[30]

Table 2. Operational and Bonus Grants Awarded to State High Risk Pools, FY2006

State	Operational Grants ($)	Bonus Grants ($)	Total Grant Award ($)
Alabama	1,442,972	0	1,442,972
Alaska	790,482	895,640	1,686,122
Arkansas	1,253,047	55,900	1,308,947
Colorado	1,658,396	1,478,373	3,136,769
Connecticut	1,147,452	700,000	1,847,452
Idaho	960,424	0	960,424
Illinois	2,939,767	1,250,000	4,189,767
Indiana	1,926,155	942,000	2,868,155
Iowa	994,340	0	994,340
Kansas	1,031,608	295,000	1,326,608
Kentucky	1,406,506	975,000	2,381,506
Louisiana	1,354,951	992,713	2,347,664
Maryland	1,797,813	1,200,000	2,997,813
Massachusetts	414,569	0	414,569
Minnesota	3,664,879	2,000,000	5,664,879
Mississippi	1,392,593	449,202	1,841,795
Missouri	1,409,440	1,000,000	2,409,440
Montana	1,074,800	729,875	1,804,675
Nebraska	1,273,440	934,097	2,207,537
New Hampshire	826,355	782,644	1,608,999
New Mexico	1,121,553	950,000	2,071,553
North Dakota	867,573	0	867,573
Oklahoma	1,388,788	1,000,000	2,388,788
Oregon	2,375,581	1,500,000	3,875,581
South Carolina	1,278,624	700,000	1,978,624
South Dakota	785,577	312,851	1,098,428
Texas	7,237,175	2,000,000	9,237,175
Utah	1,162,603	1,250,000	2,412,603
Washington	1,575,759	856,705	2,432,464
Wisconsin	2,672,935	1,750,000	4,422,935
Wyoming	773,843	0	773,843

Sources: Grant data available at http://www.cms.hhs.gov/HighRiskPools/Downloads/grantawardslist1106.pdf.

Table 3. Combined Operational and Bonus Grants Awarded to State High Risk Pools, FY2008

State	Total Grant Award ($)
Alabama	1,383,432
Alaska	686,427
Arkansas	923,943
Colorado	1,810,579
Connecticut	1,179,518
Idaho	966,948
Illinois	2,997,696
Indiana	1,706,495
Iowa	713,258
Kansas	1,085,624
Kentucky	1,688,275
Louisiana	1,437,094
Maryland	2,301,233
Minnesota	3,442,001
Mississippi	1,414,808
Missouri	1,491,340
Montana	1,054,073
Nebraska	1,195,503
New Hampshire	882,252
New Mexico	1,440,929
North Dakota	703,531
Oklahoma	1,392,608
Oregon	2,680,650
South Carolina	1,444,730
South Dakota	724,609
Texas	6,276,063
Utah	1,393,329
Washington	1,617,258
Wisconsin	2,561,169
Wyoming	504,125

Sources: Grant data available at http://www.cms.hhs.gov/HighRiskPools/Downloads/2008HRPAWARDS.pdf.

Table 4. Operational and Bonus Grants Awarded to State High Risk Pools, FY2009

State	Operational Grants ($)	Bonus Grants ($)	Total Grant Award ($)
Alabama	1,305,753	0	1,305,753
Alaska	764,558	433,684	1,198,242
Arkansas	1,240,960	689,866	1,930,826
Colorado	1,876,773	1,030,186	2,906,959
Connecticut	1,095,579	611,639	1,707,218
Idaho	908,588	511,022	1,419,610
Illinois	3,145,153	1,711,886	4,857,039
Indiana	1,749,210	962,638	2,711,848
Iowa	1,059,056	0	1,059,056
Kansas	1,011,026	566,202	1,577,228
Kentucky	1,409,657	780,200	2,189,857
Louisiana	1,313,112	730,550	2,043,662
Maryland	2,382,726	1,298,566	3,681,292
Minnesota	3,093,491	1,674,622	4,768,113
Mississippi	1,303,254	723,282	2,026,536
Missouri	1,407,332	780,031	2,187,363
Montana	995,050	556,609	1,551,659
Nebraska	1,185,291	658,054	1,843,345
New Hampshire	832,225	469,865	1,302,090
New Mexico	1,436,380	793,190	2,229,570
North Carolina	990,004	510,002	1,500,006
North Dakota	811,220	458,182	1,269,402
Oklahoma	1,291,014	717,771	2,008,785
Oregon	2,278,557	1,242,546	3,521,103
South Carolina	1,323,353	735,099	2,058,452
South Dakota	762,529	432,436	1,194,965
Texas	6,781,948	3,674,808	10,456,756
Utah	1,227,955	682,260	1,910,215
Washington	1,476,637	817,459	2,294,096
Wisconsin	2,288,872	1,247,341	3,536,213
Wyoming	753,819	0	753,819

Sources: U.S. Department of Health and Human Services, "Report to Congress on the High Risk Pool Grant Program for Federal Fiscal Years 2008 and 2009," 2010.

Health Reform

The 111th Congress passed the Patient Protection and Affordable Care Act (PPACA), which President Obama signed into law (P.L. 111-148) on March 23, 2010. PPACA, as amended, requires the Secretary of Health and Human Services to establish a temporary high risk pool program, prior to 2014, to provide health insurance coverage to certain individuals with preexisting health conditions who have been uninsured for six or more months. States can run the program or elect to have the Department of Health and Human Services (HHS) operate the program in their states. The majority of states (29 states and DC) contracted to operate their own HRPs. HHS administers the HRPs in 21 states, under the Pre-Existing Condition Insurance Plan (PCIP) name.[31]

End Notes

[1] States with existing high risk pools: AL, AK, AR, CA, CO, CT, FL, ID, IL, IN, IA, KS, KY, LA, MD, MN, MS, MO, MT, NE, NH, NM, NC, ND, OK, OR, SC, SD, TN, TX, UT, WA, WV, WI, and WY.

[2] National Association of State Comprehensive Health Insurance Plans, *Comprehensive Health Insurance for High-Risk Individuals: A State-By-State Analysis,* 2008/2009. (Hereafter cited as *Comprehensive Health Insurance.*) For online information about state high risk pools, see State Coverage Initiatives, "High-Risk Pools," at http://www.statecoverage.net/matrix/high riskpools.htm.

[3] For more information about HIPAA, see CRS Report RL31634, *The Health Insurance Portability and Accountability Act (HIPAA) of 1996: Overview and Guidance on Frequently Asked Questions*, by Hinda Chaikind et al. (Hereafter cited to as *HIPAA.*)

[4] The 35th state high risk pool was established by North Carolina, which became operational in 2009.

[5] This statistic is based on estimates of the uninsured population with preexisting health conditions for each relevant state. For additional data concerning state high risk pools, see Government Accountability Office, "Health Insurance: Enrollment, Benefits, Funding, and Other Characteristics of State High-Risk Health Insurance Pools," July 22, 2009,available online at http://www.gao.gov/new.items/d09730r.pdf. (Hereafter cited as *GAO.*)

[6] For additional information about the temporary high risk pool program established under health reform, see CRS Report R41235, *Temporary Federal High Risk Health Insurance Pool Program*, by Mark Newsom. (Hereafter cited as *Temporary Program.*)

[7] For a general discussion about health insurance, see CRS Report RL32237, *Health Insurance: A Primer*, by Bernadette Fernandez.

[8] M. Pauly and A. Percy, "Cost and Performance: A Comparison of the Individual and Group Health Insurance Markets," *Journal of Health Politics, Policy and Law*, February 2000.

[9] General Accounting Office, "Private Health Insurance: Millions Relying on Individual Market Face Cost and Coverage Trade-Offs," November 1996.

[10] For example, see National Governors Association, Policy Position, "Private Sector Health Care Reform Policy," February 25, 2009. Also, see examples from advisory groups and

academia, such as the National Association of Insurance Commissioners, News Release," NAIC Applauds Extension of Federal Funding for High-Risk Pools," July 27, 2005, and M. Pauly, "How Private Health Insurance Pools Risk," National Bureau of Economic Research, Research Summary, Summer 2005.

[11] For example, see the National Association of Health Underwriters' position on high risk pools at http://www.nahu.org/government/issues/Risk_Pools/High_Risk_Pools.htm, and the Council for Affordable Health Insurance's issue brief on high risk pools at http://www.cahi.org/cahi_contents/issues/article.asp?id=489.

[12] Richard Cauchi, National Conference of State Legislatures (NCSL), "States and High Risk Pools," May 17, 2010, http://www.ncsl.org/portals/1/documents/health/HighRiskpools webinar51710.pdf. (Hereafter cited as *NCSL.*)

[13] For example, see D. Chollet, "Expanding Individual Health Insurance Coverage: Are High-Risk Pools The Answer?," *Health Affairs*, October 23, 2002, and Pollitz, et al., "Health Insurance and Diabetes: The Lack of Available, Affordable, and Adequate Coverage," *Clinical Diabetes*, vol. 23, no. 2, 2005.

[14] For example, see testimony presented by R. Pollack, Families USA, Education and the Workforce Committee Employer-Employee Relations Subcommittee hearing, "Expanding Access to Quality Health Care: Solutions for the Uninsured," July 9, 2002, and American Federation of State, County, and Municipal Employees, "Universal Health Coverage," resolution no. 14, June 26-30, 2000.

[15] By bearing risk, a high risk pool essentially functions like an insurance carrier and is responsible for paying claims. In general, the health plan's role is for administrative purposes only. The exception to this is Idaho's pool which was established as a high risk reinsurance pool, in which individual insurance carriers underwrite the insurance offered through the pool, and receive reinsurance should expenses exceed a certain amount specified in the plan design.

[16] Communicating for Agriculture and the Self-Employed, Inc., *Comprehensive Health Insurance for High-Risk Individuals: A State-By-State Analysis, Nineteenth Edition, 2005/2006*, 2005, p. 14.

[17] An assessment is a tax or fee. Some states fund the losses of their risk pools by requiring insurers across the state to pay assessments. Generally, the amount of insurers' assessment is based on their share of the total premiums sold in the state for each year. Some states also provide tax credits to these insurers, thus reducing the insurers' tax liability and enabling them to recover some or all of their expenditures on the assessments. Under the latter of these funding mechanisms, the state assumes part or all of the cost burden for the losses of the risk pools.

[18] Kaiser Family Foundation, "State High-Risk Pools: An Overview," January 2010, available online at http://www.kff.org/uninsured/upload/8041.pdf.

[19] NASCHIP, "Lifetime Maximums," http://www.naschip.org/2010/Quick%20Checks/Lifetime %20Maximums.pdf.

[20] Ibid.

[21] See *NCSL*.

[22] HIPAA also provides protections to certain people who wish to enroll in the *group* health insurance market. For more details, see *HIPAA*.

[23] The Health Coverage Tax Credit (HCTC) is a federal income tax credit that covers most of the premium for qualified health insurance for eligible taxpayers and their family members. Eligibility for the HCTC is limited to three groups of taxpayers, two of whom are individuals eligible for Trade Adjustment Assistance allowances because they lost manufacturing, service, or public agency jobs due to foreign trade or shifts in production outside the United States. The third group consists of individuals whose defined benefit pension plans were taken over by the Pension Benefit Guaranty Corporation because of financial difficulties. For additional information about the HCTC, see CRS Report RL32620, *Health Coverage Tax Credit*, by Bernadette Fernandez.

[24] NASCHIP, "Pool Membership – 2009," http://www.naschip.org/2010/Quick%20Checks/ 2009 %20Pool%20Membership.pdf.

[25] For additional information about the grant program administered by CMS, see High Risk Pool Overview, at http://www.cms.hhs.gov/HighRiskPools/.

[26] Ohio was awarded a grant to conduct a study on the feasibility of creating a high risk pool. Utah was awarded a grant to modify its existing health plan and become a newly "qualified" high risk pool.

[27] The FY2004 grantees include Massachusetts which operates a reinsurance program for the non-group market that differs from traditional high risk pools. Nonetheless, the MA program met the requirements of the federal grant program. For a more detailed discussion about the MA reinsurance program, see *Comprehensive Health Insurance*, p. 261.

[28] For additional information, see the funding announcement online at http://www.cms.hhs.gov/ HighRiskPools/Downloads/Final_FY08_HRP_announcement.pdf.

[29] U.S. Department of Health and Human Services, "Report to Congress on the High Risk Pool Grant Program for Federal Fiscal Years 2008 and 2009," 2010.

[30] To date, no grant awards have been posted by CMS.

[31] For updated information regarding implementation of this program, see *Temporary Program*.

In: High Risk Health Insurance Pools
Editor: Jenny Alvarez
ISBN: 978-1-62417-421-6

Chapter 4

HEALTH INSURANCE: ENROLLMENT, BENEFITS, FUNDING, AND OTHER CHARACTERISTICS OF STATE HIGH-RISK HEALTH INSURANCE POOLS*

United States Government Accountability Office

July 22, 2009

The Honorable Henry A. Waxman
Chairman
Committee on Energy and Commerce
House of Representatives

The Honorable John D. Dingell
Chairman Emeritus
Committee on Energy and Commerce
House of Representatives

The Honorable Frank Pallone, Jr.
Chairman

---

* This is an edited, reformatted and augmented version of the United States Government Accountability Office, GAO-09-730R, dated July 22, 2009.

Subcommittee on Health
Committee on Energy and Commerce
House of Representatives

A growing number of states—35 as of June 2009—have created high-risk health insurance pools (HRPs) primarily to provide coverage to individuals whose health status limits their access to coverage in the private individual health insurance market.[1] HRPs—typically state-run nonprofit associations—often contract with a private health insurance carrier to administer the pool and offer a range of health plan options to such individuals, who are commonly referred to as medically uninsurable.[2] Plan options vary within pools and from state to state, and like the private individual market, HRPs typically impose waiting periods for coverage of preexisting conditions to discourage medically uninsurable individuals from foregoing health insurance until they require care.[3]

Because of the higher health care costs typically incurred by medically uninsurable individuals, all pools operate at a loss. Premiums for HRP health plans are higher than for plans offered to healthy individuals in the private health insurance market; however, these premiums are capped to limit enrollees' costs and are thus insufficient to cover the costs of enrollee health care claims.[4] As a result, all HRPs supplement their revenues through various funding mechanisms, such as assessments on health insurance carriers and state general revenues.

Federal grants are also awarded to establish and fund HRPs. As part of the Trade Adjustment and Assistance Reform Act of 2002, Congress established a program to provide grants to HRPs to offset losses and establish HRPs—commonly referred to as operational and seed grants, respectively.[5] Subsequent legislation authorized funding for the program through 2010, including grants to be used for supplemental consumer benefits—commonly referred as bonus grants.[6] Since 2003, the grant program has awarded nearly $286 million to state HRPs for various purposes. The Centers for Medicare & Medicaid Services (CMS), within the Department of Health and Human Services (HHS), administers this federal grant program.

Recent health care reform proposals call for an expanded role for HRPs to enhance health insurance options for the medically uninsurable. Because of the federal funding provided to HRPs, you expressed interest in obtaining data on several aspects of each state HRP. In this chapter, we describe (1) HRP enrollment and enrollee demographics; (2) HRP plans' cost-sharing provisions, coverage restrictions, and premiums, and comparable information for certain private market health plans; and (3) HRPs' governance, expenditures, and funding.

To address our three objectives, we administered a Web-based data collection instrument (DCI) to senior officials of the 34 HRPs in operation in 2008.[7] The data obtained were generally for fiscal year 2008, although for certain questions we obtained additional historical data. Because each HRP offers multiple plan options to enrollees, in order to simplify comparisons of plan-specific cost-sharing provisions, benefits, coverage restrictions, and premiums, we limited many of our comparisons to each pool's most popular plan—i.e., the plan chosen by the most enrollees. Collectively, the most popular plans covered 41 percent of the enrollees across the 34 HRPs.[8] To ensure the clarity and precision of our DCI questions, we pretested the DCI with officials of the National Association of State Comprehensive Health Insurance Plans (NASCHIP), an organization that provides educational resources and information to assist state HRPs in their operation. We also received comments on the DCI from a CMS official involved in the HRP federal grant program. We received responses to the DCI from all 34 HRPs, although not every HRP responded to every question in the DCI. We relied on the data as reported by the HRPs and did not independently verify or evaluate these data. However, we reviewed all responses for reasonableness and consistency, and we clarified apparent irregularities by comparing the data to other sources, such as an annual compendium of HRP statistical information compiled by NASCHIP. In addition, we followed up with state HRP representatives for clarification where necessary. Based on these activities, we determined these data were sufficiently reliable for the purpose of our report.

We supplemented information obtained through the DCI with additional data and analyses. For our first objective, we estimated the number of individuals potentially eligible for HRP enrollment because they were uninsured and had one or more preexisting health condition. To do this, we used 2006 Medical Expenditure Panel Survey (MEPS) data to determine the percentage of uninsured individuals with at least one chronic condition that was diagnosed or treated in 2006. We then applied that percentage to Current Population Survey (CPS) estimates of the number of uninsured individuals in each of the 34 states with HRPs.[9,10] We assessed the reliability of the MEPS and CPS data by reviewing related documentation and by testing the MEPS data to identify outliers, missing data, and other potential sources of errors, and we determined they were sufficiently reliable for our purposes. For our second objective, we compared selected HRP benefits and coverage restrictions to those found in employer-sponsored health insurance plans by obtaining data from two annual surveys—the Kaiser Family Foundation and Health Research and Educational Trust (KFF/HRET) *Employer Health Benefits Annual Survey* and the Mercer *National Survey of Employer-Sponsored Health Plans*.[11] KFF/HRET presents annual data based on its survey of a random sample of private and public-sector employers, which it implements from July through May each year. Mercer presents annual data based on its survey of a random sample of private-sector employers, which it implements in July of each year. For each of these surveys, we reviewed the survey instruments and methodology and determined that the data were sufficiently reliable for our purposes. To compare trends in HRP premiums to those in the private health insurance market, we compared HRP premium data reported in our DCI to premium estimates for the private individual health insurance market published by America's Health Insurance Plans (AHIP)—a health insurance trade association—and for the employer-sponsored health insurance market published by KFF/HRET. Finally, for our third objective, we supplemented the HRP funding information we obtained through the DCI with CMS documentation on the federal grants and through interviews with the CMS official who manages these grants. We did not independently verify or evaluate information we received from CMS.

We conducted our work from July 2008 to June 2009 in accordance with all sections of GAO's Quality Assurance Framework that are relevant to our objectives. The framework requires that we plan and perform the engagement to obtain sufficient and appropriate evidence to meet our stated objectives and to discuss any limitations in our work. We believe that the information and data obtained, and the analysis conducted, provide a reasonable basis for any findings and conclusions in this product.

RESULTS IN BRIEF

HRP Enrollment and Demographics of Those Enrolled

- HRP enrollment—enrollees and their dependents—totaled 199,418 in the 34 HRPs in 2008. We estimated nearly 4 million additional individuals to be potentially eligible for enrollment in an HRP based on their uninsured status and preexisting health conditions.[12]
- All HRPs accepted new applicants in 2008 except for California, which had a waiting list of about 1,030, and Florida, which has been closed to new enrollment since 1991.

- The average age of HRP enrollees in 2008 was 49 years and their average length of enrollment was 3 years. Among the 6 HRPs that collected employment or income data,[13] about half of the enrollees were employed, and the average household income was about $41,000.

Enclosure I provides additional information on HRP enrollment and enrollee demographics.

HRP Cost-sharing Provisions, Coverage Restrictions, and Premiums

- In 2008, the average annual deductible for the most popular plan offered by each of the 34 HRPs was $1,593—almost three times as high as the average annual deductible of $560 among employer-sponsored health insurance plans. About 63 percent of enrollees in these most popular HRP plans had deductibles of $1,000 or greater. In comparison, almost 88 percent of enrollees in employer-sponsored plans had a deductible of under $1,000 or no deductible.
- About 18 percent of enrollees in the 34 most popular HRP plans in 2008 were in plans that did not cover maternity care and about 3 percent were in plans that did not cover mental health services. Almost all enrollees in the most popular plans had access to prescription drug and transplant coverage.
- Fifteen percent of the most popular plans (5 plans) in 2008 had annual maximum coverage limits. These annual limits ranged between $75,000 and $300,000 and averaged $175,000. By comparison, 10 percent of employer-sponsored plans had annual limits. Almost 90 percent of the most popular plans (30 plans) had lifetime dollar limits, which ranged between $500,000 and $5,000,000 and averaged $1.6 million. By comparison, 56 percent of employer-sponsored plans had lifetime limits.
- Between 2004 and 2008, average monthly HRP premiums rose by 14 percent across all plans, from $424 to $485. During the period 2004 through 2006, HRP average monthly premiums increased by 6 percent while average premiums in the employer-sponsored health insurance and the individual health insurance markets both increased by 15 percent. During the period 2007 through 2008, HRP average monthly

premiums increased by 6 percent and employer-sponsored market premiums increased by 5 percent. No comparable individual market premium data were available for these 2 years.

- Fourteen percent of all HRP enrollees received income-based premium subsidies, which were offered by 12 HRPs in 2008. The average monthly subsidy received was $261, or about 49 percent of the subsidy recipients' average monthly premium of about $538.

Enclosure II provides additional information on HRP cost-sharing provisions, coverage restrictions, and premiums.

HRP Governance, Expenditures, and Funding

- Collectively, in 2008, HRP governing boards included representatives from health insurance carriers (41 percent of board members), state government (13 percent), medical providers (9 percent), enrollees (7 percent), and employers (3 percent), among others.[14]
- Total claims paid by HRPs in 2008 were about $1.9 billion, accounting for almost 95 percent of total HRP expenditures. The average claims per enrolled individual totaled $9,437 in 2008, an increase of about 39 percent since 2003.
- In 2008, premium revenue contributed 54 percent of HRP funding, and insurance carrier assessments contributed about 23 percent.
- HRPs were awarded a total of approximately $286 million in federal grants between 2003 and 2008, according to CMS. Almost 83 percent of these funds were operational grants, almost 15 percent were bonus grants, and less than 3 percent were seed grants. Federal grants comprised less than 2 percent of total HRP funding in 2008.
- Of the $75 million in federal grants that HRPs were awarded in 2006, about 55 percent were used to cover operational losses, about 17 percent to reduce premiums, and about 14 percent to support income-based premium subsidy programs, according to reports submitted to CMS. HRPs used the rest of the funds for various purposes, such as disease management programs and reduction in cost sharing, increasing benefit coverage, and marketing and outreach.[15]

Enclosure III contains more information on HRP governance, expenditures, and funding.

Agency Comments

We provided a draft of this chapter to HHS and NASCHIP for comment. In response, HHS provided written comments, stating that our report contains a wealth of valuable information on HRPs. HHS and NASCHIP also provided technical comments, which we incorporated as appropriate.

John E. Dicken
Director, Health Care Issues

Enclosure I. HRP Enrollment and Demographics of HRP Enrollees, Fiscal Year 2008

Table 1. HRP Enrollment in 2008 and Estimate of the Potentially Eligible Population, 2005-2007 State Averages

HRP	Total HRP enrollees	Total HRP enrollees and dependents	Estimated number of individuals potentially eligible for HRP enrollment[a]
AL	2,272	2,410	79,632
AK	469	469	14,490
AR	3,079	3,079	61,110
CA	6,809	7,036	846,720
CO	8,552	8,552	100,674
CT	2,073	2,336	43,344
FL	292	292	465,948
ID	1,272	1,337	27,216
IL	16,063	16,063	218,610
IN	6,261	6,561	96,516
IA	2,732	2,732	34,524
KS	1,693	1,863	40,320
KY	4,185	4,354	71,694
LA	1,117	1,117	101,682
MD	11,366	14,691	95,886
MN	23,511	27,386	55,188
MS	3,468	3,468	68,418
MO	3,015	3,015	91,098
MT	3,016	3,016	18,900
NE	5,126	5,126	26,712
NH	1,038	1,094	17,388

Table 1. (Continued)

HRP	Total HRP enrollees	Total HRP enrollees and dependents	Estimated number of individuals potentially eligible for HRP enrollment[a]
NM	6,020	6,020	53,550
ND	1,463	1,463	8,568
OK	2,276	2,276	80,640
OR	13,953	15,318	78,246
SC	2,329	2,329	88,830
SD	669	669	10,962
TN	3,768	3,768	104,580
TX	24,170	26,908	716,562
UT	3,621	3,621	50,274
WA	3,397	3,397	97,020
WV	568	652	33,768
WI	16,284	16,284	60,480
WY	716	716	9,198
Across all HRPs	**186,643**	**199,418**	**3,968,748**

Source: GAO data collection instrument administered to all 34 HRPs operational in 2008 and analysis of data from the 2006 Medical Expenditure Panel Survey (MEPS) and U.S Census Bureau, *Income, Poverty, and Health Insurance Coverage in the United States*: 2007.

[a] GAO estimated the potentially eligible population, including dependents, by (1) determining the percentage of uninsured individuals with at least one chronic condition using 2006 MEPS data, and (2) applying that percentage to Current Population Estimates (CPS) estimates of the 3-year average uninsured population in each of the 34 states with an HRP (2005-2007). The CPS estimates are subject to sampling error of plus or minus 1.3 percent at the 90 percent confidence level. The MEPS and CPS data used were the most current available at the time we performed our work.

Table 2. HRPs with Waiting Lists or Closed to Enrollment, 2004-2008

Year	HRPs with a waiting list (maximum number of individuals on the list)	HRPs closed to enrollment
2004	Illinois (279)	Florida
2005	Illinois (173)	Florida
2006	California (864)	Florida
2007	California (232)	Florida
2008	California (1,030)	Florida

Source: GAO data collection instrument administered to all 34 HRPs operational in 2008.

Table 3. Demographics of HRP Enrollees, by State HRP, 2008

HRP	Average age (years)	Employment status[a,b] Percentage of enrollees who are:			Average household income of new enrollees[c]	Percent male	Average length of enrollment (in months)	Percent who are HIPAA-eligible[d]	Percent who are HCTC-eligible[e]
		Employed	Unemployed	Retired					
AL	51	—	—	—	—	45.6	9	100.0[f]	0.0
AK	50	—	—	—	—	48.6	50	32.4	0.0
AR	—	—	—	—	—	47.7	42	45.1	0.6
CA	—	—	—	—	—	43.7	36	—	—
CO	45	29.8	63.4	2.1	—	46.9	26	9.4	0.1
CT	47	—	—	—	—	48.4	53	49.4	0.8
FL	50	—	—	—	—	50.3	N/A[g]	0.0	0.0
ID	47	—	—	—	—	45.0	31	—	—
IL	50	—	—	—	—	44.6	47	64.3	1.4
IN	48	—	—	—	$27,500	54.9	31	37.8	0.1
IA	49	—	—	—	—	50.3	22	43.0	0.0
KS	51	—	—	—	—	44.2	42	17.9	0.2
KY	48	—	—	—	—	51.1	29	40.3	0.0
LA	50	—	—	—	—	52.8	41	60.6	0.2
MD	49	57.8	29.1	12.1	$35,000	45.6	16	30.2	1.5
MN	—	—	—	—	—	—	—	5.2	0.1
MS	51	—	—	—	—	45.0	43	36.6	—
MO	48	—	—	—	—	50.8	25	40.1	—
MT	50	—	—	—	—	45.0	42	46.3	0.1
NE	47	—	—	—	—	52.6	59	45.2	0.0
NH	47	—	—	—	—	47.3	19	25.4	1.4
NM	48	—	—	—	—	45.9	24	17.7	0.0
ND	—	—	—	—	—	—	—	2.6	0.2
OK	—	—	—	—	—	—	—	43.6	0.0
OR	46	42.5	29.5	13.0	$29,366	41.2	31	13.7	0.2
SC	50	—	—	—	—	48.0	36	66.7	1.2
SD	47	—	—	—	—	49.6	31	100.0[f]	0.0
TN	51	—	—	—	—	40.3	6	12.1	—
TX	51	—	—	—	—	46.6	42	43.1	0.1
UT	46	47.9	5.4	3.0	$70,573	40.5	60	35.0	0.0

Table 3. (Continued)

HRP	Average age (years)	Employment status[a,b] Percentage of enrollees who are: Employed	Unemployed	Retired	Average household income of new enrollees[c]	Percent male	Average length of enrollment (in months)	Percent who are HIPAA-eligible[d]	Percent who are HCTC-eligible[e]
WA	49	—	—	—	—	57.1	45	0.0	0.0
WV	49	—	—	—	—	42.1	13	—	—
WI	51	51.1	37.0	—	$54,200[h]	54.5	40	—	—
WY	51	—	—	—	—	48.0	—	0.8	—
Across all HRPs	**49[i]**	**47**	**32**	**9**	**$41,136[i]**	**47**	**36[i]**	**28**	**0.3**

Source: GAO data collection instrument administered to all 34 HRPs operational in 2008.

Legend: — = response not provided

N/A: Not applicable

Note: Information presented for enrollees only—not dependents, with the exception of Texas where dependents are counted as enrollees because they hold their own policies.

[a] Employment status was provided by five states—Colorado and Wisconsin collected these data from new enrollees only, and Maryland, Oregon, and Utah collected it from all enrollees.

[b] Percentages may not add to 100 because some enrollees may fall into other or unknown employment status categories.

[c] Average income was provided by the five HRPs that collected income data for new enrollees in 2008.

[d] HIPAA-eligible refers to those individuals who qualify for HRP enrollment because of the Health Insurance Portability and Accountability Act of 1996, which allows for portability of health coverage for those with prior group coverage.

[e] HCTC-eligible refers to those individuals who qualify for HRP enrollment because of the Health Coverage Tax Credit, which provides tax credits for health insurance premiums for certain eligible displaced workers and retirees.

[f] Pool is open to HIPAA-eligibles only.

[g] The Florida HRP has been closed to new enrollment since 1991 and, in 2008, had 292 enrollees.

[h] Income data were provided on a voluntary basis by 77 percent of new enrollees in Wisconsin.

[i] Averages are weighted based on HRP enrollment.

Enclosure II. HRP Plan Cost-sharing Provisions, Benefits, Coverage Restrictions, and Premiums

Table 4. Average Annual Deductible of Most Popular HRP Plans Compared to Employer-sponsored Plans, 2008

	Most popular HRP plans[a]	Employer-sponsored plans[b]
Average annual deductible	$1,593[c]	$560

Source: GAO data collection instrument administered to all 34 HRPs operational in 2008 and Kaiser Family Foundation and Health Research & Educational Trust, *Employer Health Benefits: 2008 Annual Survey* (Menlo Park, Calif., and Chicago, Ill.: 2008).

Note: Deductibles are for self-only coverage and in-network services.

[a] This includes the most popular HRP plan—the plan with the most enrollees—in each of the 34 HRPs. The most popular plans had a total of 76,846 enrollees, accounting for 41 percent of total HRP enrollees in 2008.

[b] Preferred provider organization plan types.

[c] Average was weighted by the number of HRP enrollees in the 33 most popular plans that had deductibles greater than zero.

Table 5. Distribution of Enrollees by Annual Deductible Level in All HRP Plans and Most Popular HRP Plans, Compared to Employer-sponsored Plans, 2008

Annual deductible	HRPs		Employer-sponsored plans[b]
	All HRP plans	Most popular HRP plans[a]	
	Percentage of total enrollees[c]	Percentage of total enrollees[c]	Percentage of covered workers in employer-sponsored plans[d]
No deductible	1.8	1.0	32.0
$1–$499	6.0	4.1	35.4
$500–$999	17.1	32.2	20.4
$1,000–$1,999	27.1	17.8	8.8
$2,000–$2,999	24.5	39.1	
$3,000–$4,999	4.6	1.7	
$5,000 or more	17.8	4.1	2.7[e]

Source: GAO data collection instrument administered to all 34 HRPs operational in 2008 and Kaiser Family Foundation and Health Research & Educational Trust,

Employer Health Benefits: 2008 Annual Survey (Menlo Park, Calif., and Chicago, Ill.: 2008).

Note: Deductibles are for self-only coverage and in-network services. Information presented for enrollees only—not dependents, with the exception of Texas where dependents are counted as enrollees because they hold their own policies.

[a] This includes the most popular HRP plan—the plan with the most enrollees—in each of the 34 HRPs. The most popular plans had a total of 76,846 enrollees, accounting for 41 percent of total HRP enrollees in 2008.

[b] Preferred provider organization plan types.

[c] Percentages do not add to 100 because HRP enrollees in supplemental insurance plans were excluded.

[d] Percentages do not add to 100 due to rounding.

[e] Data for employer-sponsored plans were only available for deductibles of $2,000 or more.

Table 6. Distribution of Enrollees in Most Popular HRP Plans, by Annual Out-of-pocket Spending Limits, 2008

Annual out-of-pocket spending limits in most popular HRP plans	Percentage of all enrollees in most popular HRP plans
Less than $2,000	29.3
$2,001–$5,000	48.5
$5,001–$7,000	15.5
$7,001–$10,000	6.6
More than $10,000	0
Total	**100**

Source: GAO data collection instrument administered to all 34 HRPs operational in 2008.

Notes: Analysis includes the most popular HRP plan—the plan with the most enrollees—in each of the 34 HRPs. The most popular plans had a total of 76,846 enrollees, accounting for 41 percent of total HRP enrollees in 2008.

Information on out-of-pocket spending limits was provided for self-only coverage and in-network services.

Information presented for enrollees only—not dependents, with the exception of Texas where dependents are counted as enrollees because they hold their own policies.

Percentages do not add to 100 due to rounding.

Table 7. Annual Out-of-pocket Spending Limit in Each State HRP's Most Popular Plan, and Costs that Could Exceed the Limit, 2008

HRP	Annual out-of-pocket spending limit	Cost-sharing features							
		Overall annual deductible	Separate hospital deductible	Separate prescription drug deductible	Separate mental health deductible	Coinsurance	Copay for prescription drugs	Copay for mental health	Copay for physician office visits
AL	N/A								
AK	$10,000	○				○			
AR	$2,000					○			●
CA	$2,500	○				○	○	○	○
CO	$2,000	○				○	●	●	●
CT	$7,500	○	●	●	●	○	●	●	●
FL	—								
ID	$10,000	●		●		○			
IL	$1,500	●				○			
IN	$1,500			●		○	●		
IA	$5,000	○				○	●		●
KS	$3,000	○				○	○		
KY	$4,000	●				○	●	●	●
LA	$9,500	○				○			
MD	$3,000	○		●		○	●		
MN	$3,000	○		○		○	○		
MS[a]	N/A	●		●		○	●		
MO	$5,000	○		○		○	○		
MT	$7,500	○				○			
NE	$3,500	○				○	●	●	●
NH	$3,500	○		●		○	●		
NM	$2,500	○				○	●	○	○
ND	$3,000	○		○		○			

Table 7. (Continued)

HRP	Annual out-of-pocket spending limit	Cost-sharing features							
		Overall annual deductible	Separate hospital deductible	Separate prescription drug deductible	Separate mental health deductible	Coinsurance	Copay for prescription drugs	Copay for mental health	Copay for physician office visits
OK	$10,000	°			•	°	•	°	
OR	$1,500	°				°	•	°	°
SC	$5,000	°				°			
SD	$3,250	°				°	•		
TN	$5,000	°				°	•		
TX	$5,500	°		•		°	•		•
UT	$2,000	°		•		°	•	°	°
WA	$1,500	°	•	•	•	°	°	•	•
WV	$3,000	•	•	•	•	°	•	•	•
WI	$3,500	°				°	•		
WY	$2,000	°		•		°	•		

Source: GAO data collection instrument administered to all 34 HRPs operational in 2008

Legend: • = Cost is not subject to the annual out-of-pocket maximum

° = Cost is subject to the annual out-of-pocket maximum

N/A = Not applicable because the most popular plan did not have an annual out-of-pocket maximum

— = Response not provided

Notes: Blank cells indicate that the cost was not a feature of the plan's cost-sharing structure.

Analysis includes the most popular HRP plan—the plan with the most enrollees—in each of the 34 HRPs. The most popular plans had a total of 76,846 enrollees, accounting for 41 percent of total HRP enrollees in 2008.

Information on out-of-pocket spending limits was provided for self-only coverage and in-network services.

[a] Mississippi does not have an overall policy regarding the out-of-pocket maximum, but it has a $5,000 out-of-pocket maximum on allowable hospital charges, after which the policy pays allowable hospital charges at 100 percent.

Table 8. Coverage of Selected Benefits Among Most Popular HRP Plans Compared to Employer-sponsored Plans, 2008

Benefit	Most popular HRP plans[a,b]		Employer-sponsored plans
	Number of plans that cover benefit	Percentage of enrollees[c] in plans that cover benefit	Percentage of workers in plans that cover benefit
Maternity care	30	82	NA
• Maternity care covered as a rider[d]	4	10	NA
Transplants	33	100[e]	NA
Mental health services	31	97	98
Prescription drugs	34	100	98

Source: GAO survey of 34 HRPs operational in 2008 and Kaiser Family Foundation and Health Research & Educational Trust, *Employer Health Benefits: 2008 Annual Survey* (Menlo Park, Calif., and Chicago, Ill.: 2008).

Legend: NA = Not available

[a] This includes the most popular HRP plan—the plan with the most enrollees—in each of the 34 HRPs. The most popular plans had a total of 76,846 enrollees, accounting for 41 percent of total HRP enrollees in 2008.

[b] Information is for in-network services and individual (not family) coverage only. Supplemental insurance policies are excluded.

[c] Information presented for enrollees only—not dependents, with the exception of Texas where dependents are counted as enrollees because they hold their own policies.

[d] Private individual health insurance plans may offer optional coverage of additional services, such as maternity care. This extra coverage is referred to as an optional rider.

[e] The percentage of enrollees with coverage of transplants was 99.7, which rounds to 100.

Table 9. Selected Cost-sharing Features and Coverage Limits Among Most Popular HRP Plans Compared to Employer-sponsored Plans, 2008

Cost-sharing features and limits on coverage	Most popular HRP plans[a,b]		Employer-sponsored plans
	Number of plans	Percentage of enrollees in plans with feature and/or limit[c]	Percentage of covered workers in plans with feature and/or limit[d]
Separate cost sharing for inpatient hospital care, in addition to the overall plan deductible	21	56	79
Preventive services exempt from plan deductible	15	57	89
Separate prescription drug deductible for plans that cover prescription drugs	13	41	11
Required coinsurance for prescription drugs for plans that cover prescription drugs	26	76	NA
Out-of-pocket annual maximums that apply to cost sharing for prescription drugs for plans that cover prescription drugs	9	18	11
Thirty or less mental health outpatient visits covered in a year by plans that cover mental health benefits	13[e]	19	59[f]
Additional cost sharing for emergency room care	12	49	NA

Source: GAO data collection instrument administered to all 34 HRPs operational in 2008 and Kaiser Family Foundation and Health Research & Educational Trust, *Employer Health Benefits: 2008 Annual Survey* (Menlo Park, Calif., and Chicago, Ill.: 2008).

Legend: NA = Not available

[a] This includes the most popular HRP plan—the plan with the most enrollees—in each of the 34 HRPs. The most popular plans had a total of 76,846 enrollees, accounting for 41 percent of total HRP enrollees in 2008.

[b] Information is for in-network services and individual (not family) coverage only. Supplemental insurance policies are excluded.

[c] Information presented for HRP enrollees only—not dependents, with the exception of Texas where dependents are counted as enrollees because they hold their own policies.

[d] Preferred provider organization plan types.

[e] Such limits may apply to some mental health services only. For example, the New Mexico HRP reported that its mental health limits apply only to chemical dependency services.

[f] Information for mental health outpatient visits is for covered workers with outpatient mental health coverage and not specified for in- or out-of-network coverage.

Table 10. Annual and Lifetime Dollar Limits Among Most Popular HRP Plans Compared to Employer-sponsored Plans, 2008

Type of Limit	Most popular HRP plans[a,b]					Employer-sponsored plans
	Average limit	Range in limits	Number of enrollees[c] who met limit	Number of plans with limit	Percentage of plans with limit	Percentage of employer-sponsored plans with limit[d]
Annual dollar limit	\$175,000	\$75,000–300,000	10	5[e]	15	10
Lifetime dollar limit	\$1.6 million	\$500,000–5 million	16	30[f]	88	56[g]

Source: GAO data collection instrument administered to all 34 HRPs operational in 2008 and Mercer, *National Survey of Employer-Sponsored Health Plans*, 2008.

[a] This includes the most popular HRP plan—the plan with the most enrollees—in each of the 34 HRPs. The most popular plans had a total of 76,846 enrollees, accounting for 41 percent of total HRP enrollees in 2008.

[b] Information is for in-network services and individual (not family) coverage only. Supplemental insurance policies are excluded.

[c] Information presented for enrollees only—not dependents, with the exception of Texas where dependents are counted as enrollees because they hold their own policies.

[d] Among preferred provider organization and point-of-service plans offered by employers with 10 or more employees.

[e] The five HRPs that had annual limits were: California, Louisiana, Tennessee, Utah, and West Virginia. In addition, while some HRPs may not have had overall annual limits, they may have had annual limits on specific services. For example, Mississippi told us that while it did not have an overall annual limit in 2008, it had an annual pharmacy limit of \$100,000 in 2008. Similarly, New Mexico had annual limits on acupuncture, diabetic education services, therapy/rehabilitation, and annual wellness preventive benefits.

[f] HRPs may have had lifetime limits on individual services. For example, New Mexico reported that while it did not have an overall lifetime limit, it had a \$5 million lifetime limit on transplants and a \$2,500 limit on diabetic education services.

[g] Median lifetime limit was \$2,000,000.

Table 11a. HRP Average Monthly Premiums, by State HRP, 2004-2006

HRP	2004			2005			2006		
	HRP premium rate as a percent of standard market rate[a]	Average monthly HRP premium[b]	Average monthly HRP premium for 50-year-old nonsmoking male[c]	HRP premium rate as a percent of standard market rate[a]	Average monthly HRP premium[b]	Average monthly HRP premium for 50-year-old nonsmoking male[c]	HRP premium rate as a percent of standard market rate[a]	Average monthly HRP premium[b]	Average monthly HRP premium for 50-year-old nonsmoking male[c]
AL	98	$448	$358	104	$486	$412	127	$539	$478
AK	137	462	580	142	494	580	145	511	614
AR	140	463	622	140	395	389	150	419	416
CA	125	519	666	125	444	683	125	435	736
CO	144	379	689	144	376	571	134	405	622
CT	150	651	658	150	712	567	150	623	651
FL	200	—	—	200	—	—	200	—	—
ID	125	303	250	125	330	260	131	349	252
IL	138	496	610	138	517	623	137	523	660
IN	138	496	515	134	528	546	133	575	590
IA	150	681	860	150	457	329	150	471	360
KS	130	475	621	134	483	640	134	494	656
KY	130	400	324	130	424	357	130	480	369
LA	184	609	483	183	535	529	183	575	482
MD	147	272	267	131	306	273	121	283	273
MN	112	308	382	120	342	359	123	380	315
MS	150	356	316	150	375	322	150	400	366
MO	175	382	338	168	251	355	168	417	396
MT	117	349	311	134	395	358	138	426	383
NE	135	488	401	135	510	435	135	510	434
NH	140	459	458	136	477	505	125	424	498
NM	—	420	625	—	374	407	147	250	407
ND	135	304	378	135	336	402	135	363	420
OK	150	497	674	150	418	674	150	545	848
OR	102	391	482	111	344	434	110	376	506

HRP	2004			2005			2006		
	HRP premium rate as a percent of standard market rate[a]	Average monthly HRP premium[b]	Average monthly HRP premium for 50-year-old nonsmoking male[c]	HRP premium rate as a percent of standard market rate[a]	Average monthly HRP premium[b]	Average monthly HRP premium for 50-year-old nonsmoking male[c]	HRP premium rate as a percent of standard market rate[a]	Average monthly HRP premium[b]	Average monthly HRP premium for 50-year-old nonsmoking male[c]
SC	200	734	—	200	835	665	200	878	737
SD	150	139	377	150	380	429	150	404	471
TN	—	—	—	—	—	—	—	—	—
TX	200	479	397	200	489	420	200	510	456
UT	125	355	369	141	404	434	142	443	497
WA	120	416	582	120	524	777	113	514	791
WV	—	—	—	148	830	474	140	595	512
WI[d]	140	—	360	140	442	417	144	474	437
WY	150	669	711	174	675	782	179	801	899
Average monthly premium across all HRPs[e]		**$424**			**$431**			**$450**	

Source: GAO data collection instrument administered to all 34 HRPs operational in 2008.

Legend: — = response not provided

[a] In general, each HRP sets premiums as a percentage of a standard market rate, which is based on the premium rates charged by other private individual market health insurance carriers offering coverage in its state.

[b] HRPs calculated average premiums by dividing the total premium revenue in each year by the average number of enrollees for the year, with the exception of Texas which also included dependents in its calculation because they hold their own policies. The calculation excludes supplemental plans.

[c] Average premium is for a 50-year-old nonsmoking male with self-only coverage who is enrolled in that state's most popular plan—the one with the most enrollees.

[d] Wisconsin does not set its premiums as a percent of the standard rate.

[e] Averages are weighted based on HRP enrollment.

Table 11b. HRP Average Monthly Premiums, by State HRP, Continued, 2007-2008

HRP	2007			2008		
	HRP premium rate as a percent of standard market rate[a]	Average monthly HRP premium[b]	Average monthly HRP premium for 50-year-old nonsmoking male[c]	HRP premium rate as a percent of standard market rate[a]	Average monthly HRP premium[b]	Average monthly HRP premium for 50-year-old nonsmoking male[c]
AL	126	$556	$502	123	$571	$540
AK	145	563	689	140	596	761
AR	150	445	450	150	447	462
CA	125	410	717	125	471	772
CO	130	329	478	128	351	524
CT	150	628	717	150	709	802
FL	200	455	—	200	—	—
ID	125	350	247	125	367	275
IL	137	551	693	137	608	721
IN	130	598	613	129	629	613
IA	150	461	375	150	472	384
KS	134	531	681	134	589	521
KY	130	499	384	130	502	388
LA	182	527	441	180	562	482
MD	117	278	280	105	270	431
MN	119	385	325	120	410	375
MS	150	432	383	146	428	383
MO	170	453	437	150	474	450
MT	130	411	394	135	486	397
NE	135	539	564	135	502	546
NH	125	438	538	125	461	580
NM	138	245	407	137	240	407
ND	135	394	478	135	421	478
OK	150	534	848	150	552	848

HRP	2007			2008		
	HRP premium rate as a percent of standard market rate[a]	Average monthly HRP premium[b]	Average monthly HRP premium for 50-year-old nonsmoking male[c]	HRP premium rate as a percent of standard market rate[a]	Average monthly HRP premium[b]	Average monthly HRP premium for 50-year-old nonsmoking male[c]
OR	117	344	419	113	398	503
SC	200	836	693	200	926	792
SD	150	466	502	150	504	571
TN	150	670	649	150	672	649
TX	200	540	493	200	593	565
UT	137	448	542	134	444	569
WA	113	505	777	113	538	801
WV	140	608	538	130	585	466
WI[d]	149	492	429	120	466	404
WY	200	855	811	166	752	811
Average monthly premium across all HRPs[e]		**$460**			**$485**	

Source: GAO data collection instrument administered to all 34 HRPs operational in 2008.

Legend: — = response not provided

[a] In general, each HRP sets premiums as a percentage of a standard market rate, which is based on the premium rates charged by other private individual health insurance carriers offering coverage in its state.

[b] HRPs calculated average premiums by dividing the total premium revenue in each year by the average number of enrollees for the year, with the exception of Texas which also included dependents in its calculation because they hold their own policies. The calculation excludes supplemental plans.

[c] Average premium is for a 50-year-old nonsmoking male with self-only coverage who is enrolled in that state's most popular plan—the one with the most enrollees.

[d] Wisconsin does not set its premiums as a percent of the standard market rate.

[e] Averages are weighted based on HRP enrollment.

Table 12. Change in Average Monthly Premiums for all HRPs Compared to Private Health Insurance Market Premiums, 2004 to 2008

	2004 through 2006			2007 through 2008			2004 through 2008
	2004	2006	Percentage change	2007	2008	Percentage change	Percentage change
Employer-sponsored market	$308	$354	15	$373	$392	5	27
Individual market[a]	$189	$218[b]	15	NA	NA	NA	NA
HRP[c,d]	$424	$450	6	$460	$485	6	14

Sources: GAO data collection instrument administered to all 34 HRPs operational in 2008; America's Health Insurance Plans (AHIP) Center for Policy and Research, *Individual Health Insurance: A Comprehensive Survey of Affordability, Access, and Benefits, August 2005*, (Washington, D.C.: 2005), and *Individual Health Insurance 2006-2007: A Comprehensive Survey of Premiums, Availability, and Benefits* (Washington, D.C.: 2007); Kaiser Family Foundation and Health Research & Educational Trust, *Employer Health Benefits: 2004, 2006, 2007, and 2008 Annual Surveys* (Menlo Park, Calif., and Chicago, Ill.: 2004, 2006, 2007, and 2008 respectively).

Legend: NA = Not available

[a] According to model legislation prescribed by the National Association of Insurance Commissioners, an HRP should consider basing premiums on the standard market rates charged in the individual market in its state.

[b] AHIP individual market premium data are mostly as of December 2006 and January 2007.

[c] HRPs calculated average premiums by dividing the total premium revenue in each year by the average number of enrollees for the year, with the exception of Texas which also included dependents in its calculation because they hold their own policies. The calculation excludes supplemental plans. In addition, monthly averages were weighted by the number of enrollees across all plans that responded.

[d] Table shows rounded numbers for average monthly HRP premiums. However, percentage change numbers were calculated using non-rounded numbers.

Table 13. Income-based Premium Subsidies Offered by HRPs, 2008

HRP	Subsidy recipients	Maximum household income eligible for a subsidy as percentage of FPL[a]	Average discount as a percentage of monthly premium	Average monthly discount	Maximum discount available as a percentage of monthly premium
CO	3,232	481	30	$111	31
IN	238	200	40	348	45
MD	4,614	300	55	191	63
MN[b]	2,390	220	—	—	—
MT	336	150	45	266	45
NM	2,637	399	67	239	75
OR	4,729	185	—	397	95
TN	3,342	350	63	436	90
UT	795	300	37	168	50
WA	11	300	18	168	21
WI[c]	3,299	—	33	169	43
WY	92	250	30	—	33
Across all HRPs	**25,715[d]**	**285%**	**49%[e]**	**$261[e]**	**66[e]**

Source: GAO data collection instrument administered to all 34 HRPs operational in 2008.

Legend: — = response not provided

Note: Information presented for the 12 HRPs that reported that they provided income-based premium subsidies. Other HRPs may also offer income-based subsidies that are not related to premiums.

[a] Federal Poverty Level (FPL).

[b] Minnesota's subsidy program is not tied directly to the amount of premium or percent of premium an enrollee pays; rather, it is a program that provides a subsidy once a year. If enrollees qualify at 220 percent of the FPL based on household size, they receive one check per enrollee and dependent. They are not required to use these funds toward premium payment. For example, funds can be used for other purposes such as paying coinsurance, or deductible amounts due to providers. The program includes enrollees and dependents on all plans including Medicare.

[c] The income limit for Wisconsin's subsidy program was not expressed relative to the FPL, but to a level of household income. In calendar year 2008, the maximum income eligible was $25,000.

[d] Fourteen percent of all HRP enrollees were receiving income-based premium subsidies.

[e] Average is weighted by number of subsidy recipients.

Table 14. Income-based Premium Subsidy Recipients by Deductible Level, 2008

Deductible level	Number of subsidy recipients enrolled
No deductible	229
$1 – $499	2,218
$500 – $999	9,186
$1,000 – $1,999	5,851
$2,000 – $2,999	3,348
$3,000 – $4,999	909
$5,000 or more	1,538

Source: GAO data collection instrument administered to all 34 HRPs operational in 2008.

Note: Information presented for the 12 HRPs that reported that they provided income-based premium subsidies. Deductible information was not provided for all subsidy recipients.

ENCLOSURE III. HRP GOVERNANCE, EXPENDITURES, AND FUNDING

Table 15. Composition of HRP Boards of Directors Across All 34 HRPs, 2008

Group	Voting members as a percentage of total	Nonvoting members as a percentage of total
Employers	3	5
Enrollees	7	0
Insurance carriers	41	2
Medical providers	9	15
State government	13	54
Other[a]	27	24

Source: GAO data collection instrument administered to all 34 HRPs operational in 2008.

[a] Other members of HRP boards of directors include members of insurance and medical representative associations, the general public, and disability agents, among others.

Table 16. Composition of Boards of Directors by State HRP, 2008

HRP	Employers		Enrollees		Insurance carriers		Medical providers		State government		Other[a]	
	Voting	Nonvoting	Voting	Nonvoting	Voting	Nonvoting	Voting	Nonvoting	Voting	Nonvoting	Voting	Nonvoting
AL					2				3		1	
AK					5						2	
AR			1		4		1				1	
CA											5	3
CO			2		4		1			3		
CT					9							
FL			1		1		1					
ID					4				3		4	
IL									3	4	10	
IN			2		4		1		2			
IA					7				1		3	3
KS			1		6		1				3	
KY									1	1		
LA	1		1		1		2			3	5	
MD	1				1				4		3	
MN	1		2		6						2	
MS					3		1			2	3	
MO					3		2		1	4	3	
MT			1		7							

Table 16. (Continued)

HRP	Employers		Enrollees		Insurance carriers		Medical providers		State government		Other[a]	
	Voting	Nonvoting	Voting	Nonvoting	Voting	Nonvoting	Voting	Nonvoting	Voting	Nonvoting	Voting	Nonvoting
NE			1		4						2	
NH	1				6		1			1	2	
NM					4		1		1		5	
ND					3				5			
OK			1		5		1				2	
OR					5		1		1		2	1
SC					5						3	
SD		2			1	1	1	6	5	2		3
TN	2				2		2		5		2	
TX			2		2		2				3	
UT	1		1		2		1		2		5	
WA	2		2		4		1			1	1	
WV					2		1				3	
WI	1		2		4		4			1	2	
WY					3				1		3	

Source: GAO data collection instrument administered to all 34 HRPs operational in 2008.

[a] Other members of HRP boards of directors include members of insurance and medical representative associations, the general public, and disability agents, among others.

Table 17. Expenditures by State HRP, 2003 and 2008 (dollars in thousands)

HRP	Year	Paid claims				Administrative expenses[b]	Other expenditures	Total expenditures[c]
		Medical	Mental health services[a]	Prescription drugs	Total claims			
AL	2003	$23,991	—	—	$23,991	$263	$19	$24,272
	2008	21,225	—	—	21,225	363	24	21,612
AK	2003	5,749	—	$909	6,658	416	95	7,168
	2008	4,558	$54	780	5,392	352	163	5,906
AR	2003	21,375	—	—	21,375	2,149	27	23,551
	2008	19,635	—	—	19,635	2,386	—	22,021
CA	2003	97,565	—	—	97,565	4,850	—	102,415
	2008	39,201	—	—	39,201	2,507	—	41,708
CO	2003	24,876	—	5,568	30,444	3,007	—	33,451
	2008	51,401	—	11,227	62,628	5,302	—	67,930
CT	2003	22,391	—	—	22,391	725	1,164	24,281
	2008	28,108	—	7,543	35,651	521	1,098	37,270
FL	2003	4,371	—	0	4,371	552	—	4,923
	2008	2,812	—	865	3,676	630	—	4,306
ID	2003	5,715	0	0	5,715	143	32	5,889
	2008	12,578	0	0	12,578	1,360	141	14,079

Table 17. (Continued)

HRP	Year	Paid claims				Administrative expenses[b]	Other expenditures	Total expenditures[c]
		Medical	Mental health services[a]	Prescription drugs	Total claims			
IL	2003	81,814	—	25,245	107,059	6,131	—	113,191
	2008	115,607	—	40,521	156,128	8,883	—	165,011
IN	2003	90,429	0	18,617	109,046	4,538	596	114,180
	2008	57,100	0	39,810	96,910	3,991	587	101,488
IA	2003	—	—	—	1,795	365	—	2,160
	2008	25,760	307	5,392	31,459	1,442	201	33,101
KS	2003	11,488	—	1,485	12,974	318	137	13,429
	2008	19,334	—	2,930	22,264	322	852	23,438
KY	2003	10,697	91	3,802	14,591	1,281	41	15,914
	2008	31,091	527	15,654	47,272	3,122	39	50,433
LA	2003	12,174	0	1,570	13,744	746	338	14,828
	2008	7,785	0	1,791	9,576	1,137	381	11,094
MD	2003[d]	0	0	0	0	96	169	266
	2008	75,829	1,817	28,866	106,511	6,568	800	113,880
MD	2003[d]	0	0	0	0	96	169	266
	2008	75,829	1,817	28,866	106,511	6,568	800	113,880
MD	2003[d]	0	0	0	0	96	169	266
	2008	75,829	1,817	28,866	106,511	6,568	800	113,880

HRP	Year	Paid claims				Administrative expenses[b]	Other expenditures	Total expenditures[c]
		Medical	Mental health services[a]	Prescription drugs	Total claims			
MN	2003	—	—	—	175,049	9,079	0	184,128
	2008	195,904	—	49,869	245,773	10,207	1,559	257,540
MS	2003	17,956	277	5,524	23,757	1,371	0	25,129
	2008	16,260	132	6,625	23,018	1,597	0	24,615
MO	2003	11,666	—	5,062	16,728	2,114	0	18,842
	2008	16,407	—	8,387	24,794	2,849	0	27,644
MT	2003	10,369	—	3,481	13,850	1,085	112	15,047
	2008	20,968	—	4,539	25,507	1,165	209	26,882
NE	2003	32,214	0	12,657	44,871	2,891	93	47,856
	2008	39,092	0	15,827	54,920	2,982	675	58,576
NH	2003	1,499	—	60	1,559	323	42	1,925
	2008	10,997	83	1,103	12,183	702	142	13,027
NM	2003	7,136	—	2,924	10,060	425	225	10,710
	2008	46,283	381	14,189	60,853	2,454	975	64,282
ND	2003	—	—	—	8,090	281	—	8,370
	2008	—	—	—	10,343	379	—	10,722
OK	2003	16,368	0	6,993	23,361	1,227	0	24,587
	2008	16,013	0	8,320	24,333	1,239	0	25,571
OR	2003	45,624	1,508	13,961	61,092	3,976	0	65,069
	2008	125,324	7,252	30,453	163,029	7,982	0	171,011

Table 17. (Continued)

HRP	Year	Paid claims				Administrative expenses[b]	Other expenditures	Total expenditures[c]
		Medical	Mental health services[a]	Prescription drugs	Total claims			
SC	2003	18,973	—	—	18,973	1,405	275	20,652
	2008	26,630	—	—	26,630	1,737	66	28,433
SD	2003	—	—	—	—	—	—	—
	2008	3,707	—	1,518	5,225	389	0	5,614
TN	2003	0	0	0	0	0	0	0
	2008	20,443	0	4,675	25,118	2,359	0	27,477
TX	2003	124,682	—	52,696	177,378	14,284	0	191,662
	2008	182,337	—	80,210	262,547	13,715	0	276,262
UT	2003	12,275	—	3,808	16,083	1,340	—	17,424
	2008	21,021	—	4,975	25,996	1,782	—	27,778
WA	2003	—	—	—	37,493	1,746	0	39,239
	2008	30,880	838	23,490	55,208	3,567	0	58,775
WV	2003	0	—	0	0	0	0	0
	2008	1,957	—	722	2,679	387	0	3,066
WI	2003	—	—	—	110,444	4,574	0	115,018
	2008	123,458	—	33,364	156,822	6,530	0	163,352
WY	2003	4,568	—	—	4,568	51	112	4,731
	2008	7,511	—	—	7,511	74	314	7,899

HRP	Year	Paid claims				Administrative expenses[b]	Other expenditures	Total expenditures[c]
		Medical	Mental health services[a]	Prescription drugs	Total claims			
Total	2003	715,965	1,876	164,364	1,215,075	71,752	3,479	1,290,306
	2008	1,417,216	11,391	443,646	1,882,595	100,982	8,226	1,991,803
Percent change[e]		+99		+170	+55	+41	+136	+54

Source: GAO data collection instrument administered to all 34 HRPs operational in 2008.

Legend: — = response not provided

[a] Where mental health services claims are not provided, they are included in the medical claims.

[b] May include third-party administrative fees, actuarial fees, legal fees, agent fees, etc.

[c] Totals may not add due to rounding.

[d] The Maryland HRP did not begin providing health insurance coverage until fiscal year 2004.

[e] While this table presents expenditure figures in rounded numbers (thousands), the percentage change numbers were calculated based on non-rounded expenditure numbers.

Table 18. Average Claims per Enrolled Individual, by State HRP, 2003 and 2008

HRP	2003	2008
AL	$6,114	$8,807
AK	13,755	11,496
AR	6,485	6,377
CA	12,609	5,572
CO	6,251	7,323
CT	9,778	15,262
FL	8,406	12,590
ID	4,369	9,407
IL	6,668	9,720
IN	11,355	13,864
IA	13,806	11,515
KS	7,618	11,951
KY	5,939	10,857
LA	10,047	8,573
MD	0[a]	7,250
MN	5,194	8,974
MS	5,603	6,637
MO	6,856	8,224
MT	4,553	8,457
NE	7,274	10,714
NH	9,868	11,137
NM	8,383	10,108
ND	4,479	7,070
OK	8,211	10,691
OR	6,180	10,643
SC	10,546	11,434
SD	—[b]	7,810
TN	—[c]	6,666
TX	7,189	9,757
UT	5,661	7,179
WA	14,138	16,252
WV	—[d]	4,109
WI	6,330	9,630
WY	7,016	10,490
Across all HRPs	**$ 6,795[e]**	**$9,437[e]**

Source: GAO data collection instrument administered to all 34 HRPs operational in 2008 and GAO analysis of data from the National Association of State Comprehensive Health Insurance Plans, *Comprehensive Health Insurance for High-Risk Individuals: A State-by-State Analysis, 2008/2009.*

Legend: — = response not provided

Note: GAO calculated average claims based on an analysis of total claims and total enrollment—including dependents—for all state HRPs except for Indiana, which directly provided us average claims data.

[a] Maryland's HRP was first established in 2003.

[b] South Dakota's HRP was first established in 2003.

[c] Tennessee's HRP did not exist in 2003.

[d] West Virginia's HRP did not exist in 2003.

[e] Averages weighted by total enrollment.

Table 19. Sources of HRP Funding Nationwide, 2003 and 2008 (in thousands)

Type of funding	2003		2008	
	($)	Percentage of total funding	($)	Percentage of total funding
Premiums	763,850	57.4	981,882	54.0
Assessments on health insurance carriers	428,288	32.2	422,815	23.2
Other assessments	28,137	2.1	135,073	7.4
State general revenues	16,683	1.3	93,426	5.1
State tobacco tax	40,000	3.0	39,771	2.2
Federal grants[a]	1,844	0.1	31,487	1.7
Other	52,248	3.9	115,063	6.3
Total	**1,331,050**	**100**	**1,819,517**	**100[b]**

Source: GAO data collection instrument administered to all 34 HRPs operational in 2008.

[a] Federal grants were awarded by the Centers for Medicare & Medicaid Services.

[b] Totals do not sum to 100 percent due to rounding.

Table 20. Sources of Funding by State HRP, 2003 and 2008

HRP	Year	Percentage of total funding							Total funding for state HRP (in thousands)
		Premiums	Assessments on carriers	Other assessments	State general revenue	State tobacco tax	Federal grants[a]	Other	
AL	2003	65.5	33.9	0	0	0	0	0.6	$28,683
	2008	72.4	20.3	0	0	0	6.3	1.0	23,071
AK	2003	43.5	56.4	—	—	—	—	0.1	5,939
	2008	52.3	38.9	—	—	—	8	0.7	6,420
AR	2003	61.9	38.1	0	0	0	0	0.1	26,462
	2008	76.7	21.6	0	0	0	0.1	1.6	20,963

Table 20. (Continued)

HRP	Year	Percentage of total funding							Total funding for state HRP (in thousands)
		Premiums	Assessments on carriers	Other assessments	State general revenue	State tobacco tax	Federal grants[a]	Other	
CA	2003	63.4	0	0	0	36.6	0	0	109,285
	2008	45.0	0	11.2	0	43.8	0	0	88,927
CO	2003	67.1	11.9	0	0	0	0	21.0	30,640
	2008	44.8	0	0	0	0	2.5	52.7	73,399
CT	2003	62.8	31.3	—	—	—	5.9	—	25,489
	2008	59.5	37.3	—	—	—	3.3	—	36,205
FL	2003	44.1	55.9	0	0	0	0	0	4,909
	2008	51.4	44.0	0	0	0	4.6	0	3,273
ID	2003	73.4	—	—	26.0	0	0	0.6	5,889
	2008	43.2	—	—	43.5	0	6.9	6.5	14,079
IL	2003	77.2	20.6	0	0	0	0	2.2	95,167
	2008	73.3	12.9	0	12.5	0	0	1.3	154,297
IN	2003	39.2	60.7	0	0	0	0	0.1	129,245
	2008	53.3	11.1	0	33.5	0	1.8	0.4	94,616
IA	2003	27.5	72.3	—	—	—	—	0.2	4,135
	2008	57.1	38.8	—	—	—	2.6	1.4	27,031
KS	2003	76.0	23.3	0	0	0	0	0.6	13,049
	2008	49.5	43.7	0	0	0	4.2	2.6	23,754
KY	2003	23.9	21.6	0	0	0	0	54.4	40,249
	2008	42.1	21.2	0	0	0	2.7	34.1	60,431
LA	2003	50.6	31.4	4.2	11.6	0	0	2.3	17,219
	2008	48.7	10.6	3.6	12.9	0	5.6	18.6	15,512
MD	2003	0	0	72.3	0	0	0	27.7	1,723
	2008	31.4	0	61.6	0	0	1.1	5.9	133,878
MN	2003	50.7	48.9	0	0	0	0	0.3	184,128
	2008	—	—	0	0	0	74.0	26.0	4,651
MS	2003	75.1	24.1	0	0	0	0	0.8	21,623
	2008	63.8	29.5	0	0	0	3.2	3.5	28,573
MO	2003	77.2	22.7	0	0	0	0	0.1	15,809
	2008	82.1	12.6	0	0	0	3.6	1.6	25,848
MT	2003	65.6	31.6	0	0	0	2.0	0.8	16,756
	2008	65.0	29.7	0	0	3.3	0.6	1.3	25,035
NE	2003	64.7	0	0	0	0	0	35.3	48,900
	2008	52.6	0	0	0	0	2.0	45.4	58,781

HRP	Year	Percentage of total funding							Total funding for state HRP (in thousands)
		Premiums	Assessments on carriers	Other assessments	State general revenue	State tobacco tax	Federal grants[a]	Other	
NH	2003	10.2	88.4	0	0	0	0	1.4	4,794
	2008	46.1	47.4	0	0	0	4.5	2.0	13,298
NM	2003	50.6	49.1	0.1	0	0	0	0.2	11,144
	2008	23.7	74.1	0	0	0	1.4	0.8	66,210
ND	2003	66.9	33.1	0	0	0	0	0	9,050
	2008	62.7	33.9	0	0	0	3.4	0	11,797
OK	2003	56.1	43.9	0	0	0	0	0	27,759
	2008	59.8	40.2	0	0	0	0	0	25,202
OR	2003	60.0	38.5	0	0	0	0	1.5	66,864
	2008	48.9	47.2	0	0	0	1.5	2.4	167,452
SC	2003	81.4	18.5	0	0	0	0	0.1	16,929
	2008	84.5	14.1	0	0	0	0	1.3	29,719
SD	2003	—	—	—	—	—	—	—	—
	2008	70.3	14.5	0	11.9	0	0	3.3	5,930
TN	2003	—	—	—	—	—	—	—	0
	2008	26.4	0	0	72.5	0	1.1	0	30,255
TX	2003	63.8	36.0	0	0	0	0	0.2	191,662
	2008	70.5	27.7	0	0	0	1.3	0.6	276,262
UT	2003	74.4	0	0	23.3	0	0	2.2	12,498
	2008	55.6	0	0	34.9	0	4.9	4.7	30,982
WA	2003	41.3	58.7	0	0	0	0	0	31,065
	2008	30.9	66.0	0	0	0	2.6	0.5	61,664
WV	2003	—	—	—	—	—	—	—	0
	2008	60.1	0	35.3	0	0	0	4.6	5,862
WI	2003	51.4	20.1	20.3	7.9	0	0	0.3	129,118
	2008	52.5	23.1	23.5	0	0	0	0.8	169,766
WY	2003	66.9	30.8	0	0	0	0	2.3	4,869
	2008	62.8	18.8	0	15.3	0	0	3.1	6,377

Source: GAO data collection instrument administered to all 34 HRPs operational in 2008.

Legend: — = response not provided

[a] Federal grants were awarded by the Centers for Medicare & Medicaid Services (CMS). Percentages are based on awards available but may not reflect funds actually drawn down in that year. For example, according to the Minnesota HRP, it was awarded $1,984,248 in federal grants in 2003; however, these funds were not drawn down until 2004.

Table 21. Total Federal HRP Grants Awarded, 2003-2008

Type of federal grant	2003	2004	2005	2006	2007[a]	2008	Total
Operational	$38,538,311	$40,164,646	$74,989,091	$50,000,001	$0	32,669,455	**$236,361,504**
Bonus[b]	N/A	N/A	N/A	25,000,000	$0	16,457,045	**41,457,045**
Seed[c]	4,202,618	0	0	2,450,000	1,450,000	0	**8,102,618**
Total	**$42,740,929**	**$40,164,646**	**$74,989,091**	**$77,450,001**	**$1,450,000**	**$49,126,500**	**$285,921,167**

Source: Centers for Medicare & Medicaid Services (CMS).

Legend: N/A = Not applicable

[a] Only seed grants were awarded in 2007.

[b] Bonus grants were not available prior to 2006.

[c] Seed grants were awarded in 2003, 2006, and 2007.

Table 22. Cumulative Federal HRP Grants Awarded, by State HRP, 2003-2008

HRP	Type of federal grant			Total federal grants
	Operational	Bonus	Seed[a]	
Alabama	$6,571,156	$500,000	$0	$7,071,156
Alaska	4,002,711	1,065,640	0	5,068,351
Arkansas	7,195,953	145,420	0	7,341,373
California	0	0	150,000	150,000
Colorado	12,288,357	2,084,917	0	14,373,274
Connecticut	6,828,693	1,125,000	0	7,953,693
District of Columbia	0	0	150,000	150,000
Idaho	2,520,108	350,000	0	2,870,108
Illinois	24,553,892	2,397,444	0	26,951,336
Indiana	12,597,329	1,442,000	0	14,039,329
Iowa	4,157,835	0	0	4,157,835
Florida	0	0	150,000	150,000
Georgia	0	0	150,000	150,000
Kansas	4,475,963	695,000	0	5,170,963
Kentucky	9,505,610	1,725,000	0	11,230,610
Louisiana	4,562,054	1,542,713	0	6,104,767
Maryland	9,421,081	2,025,000	1,000,000	12,446,081
Massachusetts	1,704,415	0	0	1,704,415
Minnesota	15,456,436	3,250,000	0	18,706,436
Mississippi	8,206,031	974,202	0	9,180,233
Missouri	4,735,438	1,550,000	0	6,285,438
Montana	4,860,622	1,104,875	0	5,965,497
Nebraska	5,911,145	1,327,816	0	7,238,961
New Hampshire	3,732,650	1,107,644	1,000,000	5,840,294
New Mexico	7,850,167	1,500,000	0	9,350,167
New York	0	0	150,000	150,000
North Carolina	0	0	1,000,000	1,000,000
North Dakota	2,894,342	178,440	0	3,072,782
Ohio	0	0	150,000	150,000
Oklahoma	10,282,089	1,525,000	0	11,807,089
Oregon	7,958,345	2,450,000	0	10,408,345
Rhode Island	0	0	150,000	150,000
South Carolina	4,128,780	1,250,000	0	5,378,780
South Dakota	2,384,720	521,451	1,000,000	3,906,171
Tennessee	0	0	1,000,000	1,000,000
Texas	21,023,993	3,620,691	0	24,644,684
Utah	5,769,821	1,825,000	52,618	7,647,439
Vermont	0	0	1,000,000	1,000,000
Washington	4,987,098	1,466,892	0	6,453,990
West Virginia	0	0	1,000,000	1,000,000

Table 22. (Continued)

HRP	Type of federal grant			Total federal grants
	Operational	Bonus	Seed[a]	
Wisconsin	13,400,216	2,706,900	0	16,107,116
Wyoming	2,394,454	0	0	2,394,454
Total	**$236,361,504**	**$41,457,045**	**$8,102,618**	**$285,921,167**

Source: GAO analysis of Centers for Medicare & Medicaid Services (CMS) data.

[a] Certain operating HRPs were awarded seed grants. For example, Utah's HRP, which became operational in 1991, was awarded a seed grant in 2003 for program modification.

Table 23. Use of Federal HRP Operational and Bonus Grants Awarded in 2006

Grant use	2006 Grants					
	Type of federal grant				Total	Percentage of total operational and bonus federal grants
	Operational		Bonus			
	Number of HRPs	Amount	Number of HRPs	Amount		
Covering operational losses	30	$41,300,050	N/A	N/A	**$41,300,050**	55.1
Reducing premiums[a]	5	6,027,017	7	6,575,952	**12,602,969**	16.8
Income-based premium subsidy[b,c]	1	2,672,935	6	7,550,000	**10,222,935**	13.6
Reduction in cost sharing	N/A	N/A	1	1,500,000	**1,500,000**	2.0
Disease management[c]	N/A	N/A	9	5,015,126	**5,015,126**	6.7
Other[c,d]	N/A	N/A	7	4,358,923	**4,358,923**	5.8
Totals[e]		**$50,000,000**		**$25,000,000**	**$75,000,000**	

Source: GAO analysis of Centers for Medicare & Medicaid Services (CMS) data.

Legend: N/A = Not applicable

HRPs may use a certain type of grant for more than one purpose. For example, an HRP that was awarded a bonus grant may use it to reduce premiums and to expand disease management programs.

[a] According to CMS, five states—Louisiana, Missouri, South Carolina, Texas, and Wyoming—had a standard market rate for individual coverage (SRR) over 150

percent; therefore, they were required to spend 50 percent of their operational grant to reduce premiums.

[b] Wisconsin spent all of its operational grants on income-based subsidies.

[c] Oklahoma and Montana spent $1 million and $729,875 respectively on premium subsidies and disease management programs. Because we could not obtain dollar amounts separately for these two grant uses, we included them in the "other" category.

[d] Other uses include increased benefit coverage, marketing, and outreach, among others.

[e] Totals may not add due to rounding.

Table 24. Use of Federal HRP Operational and Bonus Grants, Awarded in 2006, by State HRP

HRP	Grant uses					
	Covering operational losses	Premium reduction	Income-based premium subsidy	Reduction in cost sharing	Disease management	Other[a]
Alabama	•					
Alaska	•					•
Arkansas	•				•	
Colorado	•				•	
Connecticut	•	•				
Idaho	•					
Illinois	•	•				
Indiana	•		•		•	
Iowa	•					
Kansas	•				•	
Kentucky	•				•	
Louisiana	•	•			•	•
Maryland	•		•			
Massachusetts	•					
Minnesota	•		•			
Mississippi	•				•	
Missouri	•		•			
Montana	•				•	•
Nebraska	•				•	
New Hampshire	•	•			•	•
New Mexico	•					•
North Dakota	•					

Table 24. (Continued)

HRP	Grant uses					
	Covering operational losses	Premium reduction	Income-based premium subsidy	Reduction in cost sharing	Disease management	Other[a]
Oklahoma	•				•	•
Oregon	•			•		
South Carolina	•	•				
South Dakota	•					•
Texas	•	•				
Utah	•		•			
Washington	•	•				
Wisconsin[b]			•			
Wyoming	•					
Total	**30**	**7**	**6**	**1**	**11**	**7**

Source: GAO analysis of Centers for Medicare & Medicaid Services (CMS) data.

Legend: • = grant use

Note: HRPs may use a certain type of grant for more than one purpose. For example, an HRP that was awarded a bonus grant may use it to reduce premiums and to expand disease management programs.

[a] Other uses included increased benefit coverage, marketing, and outreach, among others.

[b] Wisconsin spent all of its operational grants on income-based subsidies.

Table 25. Planned Use of Federal Operational and Bonus HRP Grants Awarded in 2008, by State HRP

HRP	Grant uses					
	Covering operational losses	Reducing premiums	Income-based premium subsidy	Reduction in cost sharing	Disease management	Other
Alabama	•	•	•			
Alaska	•					•
Arkansas	•				•	
Colorado	•				•	
Connecticut	•					•
Idaho	•					•
Illinois	•	•				
Indiana[a]	•		•			
Iowa	•					

HRP	Grant uses					
	Covering operational losses	Reducing premiums	Income-based premium subsidy	Reduction in cost sharing	Disease management	Other
Kansas	•				•	•
Kentucky	•				•	
Louisiana	•	•			•	•
Maryland	•		•			
Minnesota	•		•			
Mississippi	•				•	
Missouri	•		•			
Montana	•		•		•	
Nebraska	•				•	
New Hampshire	•	•	•		•	•
New Mexico	•		•			
North Dakota	•				•	
Oklahoma	•	•				
Oregon	•			•	•	
South Carolina	•	•				
South Dakota	•					•
Texas	•	•				
Utah	•		•			
Washington	•	•			•	
Wisconsin[b]		•	•		•	
Wyoming	•	•				
Total	**29**	**10**	**10**	**1**	**13**	**7**

Source: GAO analysis of Centers for Medicare & Medicaid Services (CMS) data.

Legend: • = grant use

[a] According to an Indiana HRP official, Indiana also used 2008 grant funds to reduce premiums and for disease management.

[b] Wisconsin planned to spend its operational grant on premium reduction.

End Notes

[1] Participants in the private individual market include self-employed people; people whose employers do not offer health insurance coverage; people not in the labor force; early retirees who no longer have employment-based coverage and are not yet eligible for Medicare; and people who lose their jobs and have exhausted or are ineligible for continuation of employer-based coverage.

[2] Individuals who—due to a preexisting health condition—have been rejected for coverage or charged higher premiums in the private individual market are typically eligible for HRP coverage. Other groups of individuals may also be eligible for HRP coverage. States may

use HRPs to implement the group market to individual market portability provision of the Health Insurance Portability and Accountability Act (HIPAA) of 1996. Pub. L. No. 104-191, title I, §111, 110 Stat. 1936, 1978. HIPAA requires that individuals with prior group coverage must have continued access to nongroup coverage with any preexisting condition waiting periods waived. In addition, states can designate HRPs as qualified health coverage for displaced workers and retirees eligible for the federal Health Coverage Tax Credit, under the Trade Adjustment Assistance Reform Act of 2002. Pub. L. No. 107-210, Div. A, §201 (a), 116 Stat. 935, 954.

[3] Most states offer waivers for the waiting period for coverage of preexisting medical conditions. Examples of criteria to qualify for a waiver often include involuntary termination of coverage by a previous carrier or previous creditable coverage within the past 12 months, among others. HIPAA-eligible enrollees are not subject to preexisting condition restrictions.

[4] Where funding is limited, an HRP may need to restrict enrollment by various means, such as by temporarily closing the pool to new enrollees or maintaining a waiting list.

[5] Pub. L. 107-210, Div. A, § 201(b), 116 Stat. 935, 959.

[6] *See*, the Deficit Reduction Act of 2005, Pub. L. 109-171, § 6202, 120 Stat. 4, 134 (2006) and the State High Risk Pool Funding Extension Act of 2006, Pub. L. 109-172, § 2, 120 Stat. 185. The State High Risk Pool Funding Extension Act authorized a total of $75 million in operational and bonus grants for each of fiscal years 2006 through 2010 and $15 million in seed grants for fiscal year 2006. Bonus grants are to be used for supplemental consumer benefits such as premium subsidies, disease management programs, and HRP expansion efforts.

[7] We did not include the North Carolina HRP in our DCI because it was not operational until 2009.

[8] In this chapter, we refer to the primary policyholders as enrollees.

[9] The MEPS and CPS data we used were the most currently available at the time we performed our work. We used the 2006 MEPS, which is a set of large-scale surveys of families and individuals, their medical providers, and employers across the United States administered by the Agency for Healthcare Research and Quality. MEPS collects information regarding individuals' demographics, health status, and insurance status, among other characteristics. We also used data published in the U.S. Census Bureau's report, *Income, Poverty, and Health Insurance Coverage in the United States: 2007*, on the 3-year average (2005-2007) of the uninsured populations by state. These data were based on the CPS Annual Social and Economic Supplement, which is a household survey that collects demographic information, such as employment and health insurance status, among other characteristics.

[10] Our estimate of individuals potentially eligible for HRP enrollment may be understated because we excluded from our MEPS analysis individuals with conditions that are not always chronic in nature or that were diagnosed or treated prior to 2006. Conversely, our estimate could be overstated to the extent it includes uninsured individuals who may not be eligible because they had access to other private or public coverage but chose not to enroll. The CPS estimates of the uninsured in each state are subject to sampling error of plus or minus 1.3 percent at the 90 percent confidence level.

[11] We compared HRP benefits and coverage restrictions to those in employer-sponsored plans because, according to model legislation prescribed by the National Association of Insurance Commissioners (NAIC), HRP plan benefit levels and deductibles should be comparable to coverage provided by large employers in the state. NAIC model legislation provides a basis for the uniform regulation of HRPs throughout the states.

[12] GAO estimated the potentially eligible population, including dependents, by (1) determining the percentage of uninsured individuals with at least one chronic condition using 2006 MEPS data, and (2) applying that percentage to CPS estimates of the 3-year average uninsured population in each of the 34 states with an HRP (2005-2007). The CPS estimates are subject to sampling error of plus or minus 1.3 percent at the 90 percent confidence level.

[13] Employment information was provided by Colorado, Maryland, Oregon, Utah, and Wisconsin. Income information was provided by Indiana, Maryland, Oregon, Utah, and Wisconsin for new enrollees only.

[14] Percentages provided are out of total voting board members. HRP governing boards may also include nonvoting members.

[15] Such funds were next awarded in 2008. Annual reports on how HRPs used these 2008 grants were not available at the time of this chapter, so they were not included in our analysis.

INDEX

I

J

K

L

M

N

O

P

R

S

T

U

V

W

X